BORN TO PLAY

BORN
TO
PLAY

MY LIFE
IN THE GAME

Dustin Pedroia

with Edward J. Delaney

G

GALLERY BOOKS

NEW YORK LONDON TORONTO SYDNEY

G

Gallery Books
A Division of Simon & Schuster, Inc.
1230 Avenue of the Americas
New York, NY 10020

First Gallery Books trade paperback edition March 2010

GALLERY Books and colophon are trademarks of
Simon & Schuster, Inc.

For information about special discounts for bulk purchases,
please contact Simon & Schuster Special Sales at
1-866-506-1949 or business@simonandschuster.com

The Simon & Schuster Speakers Bureau can bring authors
to your live event. For more information or to book an event
contact the Simon & Schuster Speakers Bureau at
1-866-248-3049 or visit our website at www.simonspeakers.com.

Designed by Joseph Rutt, Level C Design

Manufactured in the United States of America

10 9 8 7 6 5 4 3 2 1

The Library of Congress has cataloged the hardcover edition as follows:

Pedroia, Dustin.
    Born to play : my life in the game / by Dustin Pedroia with Edward J. Delaney.
        p. cm.
1. Pedroia, Dustin.   2. Baseball players—United States—Biography.
I. Delaney, Edward J.   II. Title.
    GV865.P43A3 2009
    796.357092—dc22   2009011572

ISBN 978-1-4391-5775-6
ISBN 978-1-4391-5776-3 (pbk)
ISBN 978-1-4391-6487-7 (ebook)

PHOTO CREDITS:
The Pedroia Family: 1, 2, 3, 4, 5, 6, 12, 13, 14, 17, 20, 21, 22
Arizona State University: 7, 8, 9
Nate Policar: 10
Boston Red Sox: 11, 18, 19
Pawtucket Sox: 15, 16

Acknowledgments

I wanted to share my story because I know a lot of fans will be able to relate to it in a positive way. I hope every one of you can believe that good things will happen if you work hard and believe in yourself, no matter what you want to accomplish in your life.

I hope everyone enjoys my story, and I thank all of you for reading it.

My parents sacrificed a lot and sold a lot of tires so I could play the game I love. Because of their dedication I have been able to realize my dream and enjoy success at the same time.

I want to thank my coauthor, Ted Delaney, for his tireless work. He took my words and life experiences both on and off the baseball field and brought my story to life.

Thanks to my agents, Sam and Seth Levinson, and thanks to my literary agent, Ian Kleinert.

Thanks also to my editor, Kevin Smith, and to Pam Ganley of the Boston Red Sox Media Relations office.

I want to thank everyone who participated and helped tell my story, including my wife Kelli, Terry Francona, Dave Magadan, Alex Cora, Mike Lowell, Ben Cherington, Ron Johnson, Fred Lynn, Ron McNutt, Steve Hyder, Rob Rinaldi, Mrs. Julia Ruth Stevens, and Adam Speakman.

It's impossible to mention all the people who have had an impact on my life. I only wish there was a way to thank all of you individually.

My Red Sox teammates, from the minors to the majors, have been an inspiration. We all share the same goal and that is to bring as many World Series titles to Boston as we can.

I especially want to thank Red Sox beat writer Joe McDonald, who first approached me before my rookie season in 2007 and encouraged me to share my story with the baseball world. Joe knew there'd be a good story to tell before the story even happened.

Last, and most important, I want to thank the fans. There's no better place to play than in Boston. The atmosphere at Fenway Park is a special one because Red Sox Nation is able to relate to the Red Sox players in a winning environment that will continue for a long time.

For Kelli

Contents

Prologue

He's right at the gate, and they won't let him pass. It seems that for so long, that's always been how it is.

It's Saturday, October 27, 2007, and Dustin Pedroia is once again trying to get where people don't believe he should go. It's been that way in high school and college and in the minor leagues and in the majors. And now, in the World Series, he's playing for the Boston Red Sox, who have just arrived at Denver's Coors Field to get ready for that evening's Game Three against the Colorado Rockies.

But the security guard who patrols the players' entrance isn't buying the idea that this . . . kid . . . could possibly be a major-league ballplayer.

To this guard, whose job it is to know a major leaguer from everybody else trying to crash the party, this kid is clearly another one of these wannabes. They come like this, the autograph seekers, the hangers-on, the jokers. Clearly you can tell the kinds of guys who do not belong in a big-league clubhouse. They're always trying to fake their way in, or push their way in, or talk their way in.

This guy has got to be kidding. Look at him! Too short, too slight, too young. He looks too much like a normal person, too much like the rest of us. The real players have been coming through, men with size and substance and the looks that speak of lifetimes of success upon success. There is, always, a kind of easiness to them that does not reside in the everyday people who line up at the turnstiles and pay to enter.

And now this guy's trying to slip past?

The guard isn't buying it, but the kid is still trying to push on through.

That's how it's always been, the giant talent in the small package, the looks-can-be-deceiving manner that forms itself into a swagger and an attitude. The chip on the shoulder; the in-your-face posture.

The guard at this gate wants an ID, but when he is shown it, he still can't bring himself to believe it. The anger forms in the kid's face, the voice rises.

Dustin Pedroia has come a long way to be here, and now he's this close to the dream. He's just going to push on by. He's going to make them have to stop him.

A Scout for a National League Team

(who wishes to remain anonymous)

Over the years there have been several players I didn't care for as a scout, but who later overachieved beyond whatever I thought they would do.

I've been able to run into some of them and talk to them. When I do, I'm not afraid to admit I was wrong. If the occasion ever arises with Dustin Pedroia—and I know he's a red-ass when it comes to people who doubted him—I would gladly say to him, "Listen, here's the way I looked at you and you've proved me wrong. And there are a couple of things I'd like to ask you."

Things that I've seen him do separate him from other people, and I would want to pick his brain. For instance, as good a hitter as Manny Ramirez is—and I think he might be the best right-handed hitter playing now; if not it's Albert Pujols—Ramirez still gives up at-bats at times.

Pedroia never gives up an at-bat.

He makes you work your ass off to get him out. I don't know what it is. Is it strictly his mental makeup? Or is there some approach he has that enables him to do this, something that other people don't do? He is a tough, tough out. The pitch that maybe you get him on one time, you don't get him on again, even in the same at-bat sometimes.

I would be curious, if I ever ran into him, to just talk to him about that. And couple that with the fact that, "Hey, I didn't care for you but you've done this, this, and this."

Personally, I admire that.

I know he's had to prove people wrong. But it's an admirable quality in him that he doesn't give up an at-bat. Everybody does. Everybody has horseshit at-bats. He makes you work. As a big leaguer I can see that, but I don't remember it being as prevalent when I saw him in Triple-A Pawtucket.

The major thing is, the Red Sox hype their people, and as a ball club you always hype your top-round pick. That's understandable. We, as scouts, all know that. As an example: Your first-round pick doesn't always become a big leaguer. But when you're picking your first-round pick in the draft, you'd like to think that the guy will not only reach the big leagues, but also be pretty damn good. You don't draft a pitcher in the first round and say, "Boy, I hope this guy will be a number-five starter." You just don't do that.

The point with Pedroia is, what did the Red Sox see in him? With your first pick of a draft, you have to assume you're picking a guy who can be really productive, and I can't think the Red Sox are this smart. I think Pedroia outsmarted everybody.

First of all, and I don't care what Pedroia says, his throw had a f—— arc on it going to first base from shortstop.

Now his arm doesn't show up as a second baseman. He goes to his right very well and he can plant himself and he gets more than enough on it. He's fine over there. I still don't think he can be a shortstop. And I might be wrong on that, too.

My point is, again, when they drafted him, what did they see? When I scouted him, the only tool I saw he had was the ability to hit for average. He couldn't throw. He didn't run. He wasn't an average fielder at that time. He might be a Gold Glover today, but in Pawtucket he wasn't even an average fielder. And, obviously, he didn't have average power. The only tool he had was the ability to hit for average. So for him to have value, you would look at that and say, well, how high does he have to hit?

He would have had to hit .300. Now he's exceeded that. But obviously his other tools have really improved. Nobody can quarrel with his defense today. Whatever is in his mind, that determination he has enables him to do the things he does.

He has the ability to get on top of a high fastball better than anybody.

Now, maybe when you're his height a lot of pitches are high fastballs. But my point is, other guys would just sky those balls and pop out. He can hit that ball as a line drive that's up around the letters. Not too many guys do that. I don't know how he does that. I don't know if there's somebody who has gotten a hold of him as a pro. Scouting him for my organization, we always quarreled with the fact that he swung from his ass, yet his strikeouts were low and he's made himself a tough out.

There're a lot of qualities in him where if you or I did the same things he did, we would fail. What I would like to ask him is, what has enabled him to succeed doing things contrary to what you would think? Like swinging from your ass. How does he enable himself to get on top of that high pitch? How has he been able to do these things?

It can't just be his attitude. Like trying to prove people wrong. Somebody said he compiled a list of everybody who said he would never make it and he wanted to prove them wrong. That's an admirable quality, but you still have to have ability.

He's done it. Damn, he's done it.

There's something inside him. There's something inside him that's not in other people, basically.

If a lot of his success comes from the whole idea of proving people wrong and being told he couldn't do it, can he maintain that level of intensity and wanting to get back at people for a career? He's proved everybody wrong. What's the next step?

What gets me, and it goes back to the draft, is how you make that choice. Let's think of somebody like him. If there were a person out there who I was claiming was going to be our first draft pick and if I was pushing and pushing for some guy who had one "plus tool," meaning a tool that was better than average for the majors—throwing, hitting, fielding, running—he could never be a team's first pick. That's why I don't understand how the Red Sox pulled the trigger on Pedroia.

You can easily hang your hat on a first pick with four plus tools. You couldn't do that with Pedroia. And that's why I can't figure out how the Red Sox could have picked him where they did. Knowing the way the draft works, and the way these bosses are, somebody had a lot of balls to pick anybody like that. Forget it's Dustin Pedroia; it could have been Player X.

They always used to compare Pedroia with David Eckstein. Well, obviously he's turned out to be better than that. But the point is, Eckstein wasn't a first pick, he was drafted in the nineteenth round in 1997. Eckstein turned out fine, but it just baffles me how somebody would take Pedroia as their first pick.

It would be like if you took a pitcher and you said the pitcher is a right-hander and he's in college and he throws eighty-five miles per hour and he doesn't show the makings of a very good curveball and he doesn't use his changeup very much and his control is below average, but I want to take him in the first round. People would just laugh at you.

I still don't understand it. Somebody up there in Boston must be a f—— genius.

1

Early Innings

Is it possible to have swinging a baseball bat as your earliest memory? I swear mine is.

My parents say I was still in diapers when they gave me a miniature San Francisco Giants bat, the kind of tiny bat you buy at a souvenir store. It was maybe sixteen inches long, and probably weighed six ounces.

What I have no memory of is this: I'm told I began to pick up that bat and take my cuts as if I'd just been waiting to get it in my hands. I'd swing at anything in front of me, and I'd do some damage. Chair legs, whatever. Sometimes the family pets.

We had this little goose my mother had gotten as a pet. When I was something like eighteen months old, I had my bat in my hands and I just went after that thing. It was like instinct. From what I'm told, it didn't turn out too well for the goose, unfortunately. I was a little baby and I was just swinging at everything. And then my mother made a decision that I'm definitely glad for: she decided to lose the goose and let me keep my bat.

I have no recollection of all that, but it's clear in some of my earliest memories that I was swinging that bat hard. Even then I was *raking*. This was as a really young kid, maybe four years old. I was hitting before I even knew any better. It started as kind of a joke, the way you can get little kids to get up and do something funny. Saturdays in the fall, my family would ride up from my hometown of Woodland, California, to the University of California at Berkeley to see the football games. My uncle, Phil Snow, was the secondary coach of the Cal Golden Bears, so my family never missed a home game.

We'd get to Memorial Stadium in Berkeley early and tailgate before the games. My mom and dad say I carried that bat around constantly from when I was barely able to walk. I remember that as the adults sat around, eating and talking, my brother would wad up foil balls and throw them to me. Usually at that age, kids don't have much hand-eye coordination, or really anything close to it. But Brett would throw me the foil ball and I would hit line drives everywhere.

I was like, "This is fun."

I would run around and do all kinds of stuff. I'd hit and catch and throw like I was my older brother, because Brett loved baseball. It was all just kind of funny to my parents. Everyone at the tailgate party would be saying, "Wow, your son's really good."

My parents would just laugh.

MY FAMILY IS down-to-earth, and we work hard. My grandfather Bo Pedroia was a truck driver for fifty years. To my father's side of the family, it was about being a man's man. Bo was always a big, strong guy, and I always respected him. He was a big-time authority figure. If he said, "Do this," I did it without question. And when Grandpa Bo Pedroia talks to you, he kind of puts the fear in you.

He loved playing cards. We'd go to family Thanksgivings at Bodega Bay and Grandpa Bo and I would play cards all day. And he was competitive. If he was losing, every other word out of his mouth was a curse. He's an awesome guy and he didn't care what people thought of him if he knew he was doing the right thing. I'd say he was also a little crazy.

My dad, Guy Pedroia, is the opposite of his dad. My Grandpa Bo was way more outgoing, and my dad was much more on the quiet side. He used to be a little loud when I was a kid and he had to yell at me, but as I grew up it got to a point where he didn't need to do that anymore.

When I'm asked where I got my work ethic, I just point to my parents.

What I do, playing baseball for a living, is easy compared to how hard they've worked all their lives. My parents own three tire stores around Sacramento, California. My dad has been in the tire business since he was a kid. My mother, Debbie, works there, too. They've run the business together since before I was born.

The original shop they started off with is called Valley Tire, in Woodland. It's been around for years.

Dad was a really good baseball player when he was young. But when my grandparents got divorced, my dad moved in with his mom. There really wasn't a lot of money, so when he was fourteen years old he started working at a tire shop, owned by a man named Mr. Orrick. He was working for something like $1.25 an hour. He worked there for eleven years under Mr. Orrick.

Dad worked, went to school, and played sports. He met my

mom when she worked at a coffee shop in Winters, California. It's about twenty minutes away from where my dad grew up. She was a waitress and he was just eating there; he went back every day for a month and tried to ask her out on a date. She kept turning him down until finally she said yes.

Mr. Orrick had two daughters, and neither of them wanted to take over the shop. He asked Dad if he wanted to buy it. Dad told him he wanted to but didn't have the money. So they worked out a deal where Dad would take over the shop and pay him back as soon as he could.

Because Mr. Orrick knew my dad was honest, and that he had always worked hard, he sold Dad the shop on a payment plan.

Those first years, my mom and dad would open the store at six in the morning and close it at nine at night. For years, my parents worked fifteen-hour days to keep it going and make enough both to live on and to make good on their payments—they paid off Mr. Orrick within a few years. When Brett was a little kid, he spent all day in the shop, playing while my parents worked.

When Brett was young and people asked him where he lived, he'd say "Valley Tire." I don't think he was joking.

I did my time working at the shop later on, but when I was little, all I wanted to do was play baseball, and my parents made sure that Brett and I always had that support from them.

Both sides of my family were athletes. My mother played tennis at Sacramento City College, but that ended when my parents got into a bad car accident. They were driving home from a family event and were struck by a hit-and-run driver. My mom ended up with two broken legs and a fracture in her back. That ended her tennis career. But she's an extremely good athlete, and maybe the most competitive of all of us. My mom says that when she'd lose a tennis match in college, she couldn't sleep for three or four nights after that. It was how she was. All I did was inherit that.

My mom's brother, my uncle Phil, had played college football; my dad was a good baseball player. He played softball later on, although that was just for relaxation—slow-pitch softball was about drinking a beer and then launching some bombs.

The good thing about my hometown was that it was small, and there was basically nothing to do in Woodland but play sports. Growing up, I always played baseball and basketball. I'd be tagging around with my brother and his friends, trying to play with them, because I was always beating the guys who were my own age. I figured I might as well try to beat my brother and his friends. We all had a competitive nature. I'd play my brother one-on-one all the time in basketball, and beat him, and he was always getting pissed, trying to beat me up and stuff. I thought, Wow, this is *awesome* . . .

And I just always played baseball. Once I got old enough, I played in the Woodland Little League, where my dad was a coach. My first year, I was seven years old and they had Single A, Double A, Triple A, and Majors. They started me off at Double A. My brother was a twelve-year-old, so my dad coached him and not me. It was hard to coach two teams on top of all the work he had at the shop. My brother's team was the Red Sox, and I got to be batboy. That was the first time I wore those words, when I got to wear that uniform for his games.

After all the kids did the tryouts, they had the Woodland Little League draft, and I was the first player taken. But the team I played for that first season ended up being the worst team. I think we went 2-20. I learned what it was like to lose, but right from then, I knew I didn't have to enjoy it. After the games, all the kids would want to go get ice cream or something, but I'd just be pissed. I was seven and I already had decided that losing totally sucked.

My dad used to work with Brett and me. One of his rules was that I had to take as many ground balls as swings. I always wanted to just hit. But my dad knew I needed to be a more rounded player. So if I got fifty swings at the ball, then I got down and took fifty ground balls. Or a hundred swings, then a hundred ground balls.

Dad threw a lot of pitches during my childhood years. I never got tired of swinging at them.

Because I was showing some ability, I got to go to a local hitting clinic run by a guy named Rich Chiles. He was from Sacramento and he'd played in the big leagues for the Astros, Mets, and Twins. He had a hitting facility about ten minutes from our house, and my dad would send my brother and me there for lessons.

Rich would have us hit for an hour and do all these funky drills. It was me and all these guys who were five years older than me. Right from the start, I was hitting better than all of them. And then they were all getting pissed and trying to beat me, this kid who was seven and hitting better than the twelve-year-olds. I thought that was even more awesome. My brother shrugged and told them that I was just kind of a freak.

Rich had a batting cage at his facility, and in it was one of those old "Iron Mike" pitching machines, the kind that has a long metal arm that throws the ball. The machine was set to pitch the balls at something like sixty or seventy miles an hour, which from a Little League mound was probably like a hundred-mile-an-hour pitch from a mound on a full-sized field. And I hadn't even seen a forty-mile-an-hour pitch playing in the Woodland Little League Double A, I'll tell you that.

One day, Rich had it cranked all the way up to top speed. The problem was that the pitching machine wasn't too accurate. I mean, the balls were just flying all over the place. Rich looked at us, and said for anyone who wanted to try hitting to step in. All the other kids were saying, "No way I'm getting in there!" No one was going near that cage. That Iron Mike was humming and had a basketful of baseballs, waiting for a victim.

I didn't give a shit. I figured if I got hit, it would only hurt for a couple of minutes, so I might as well go and see how I could do against fastballs.

The first few pitches from the machine came down the middle and I hit them. I was feeling pretty good, like this was no problem. Then the machine cranked out a wild pitch and it nailed me right in the back. It was my first time getting hit by a full-speed pitch.

I yelled, "F—!"

I mean, I was seven, and that thing *stung*. I think besides being the first time I got hit by a fastball, I'm also pretty sure it was the first time I ever said "f—."

It hurt for a couple of minutes, but then I got back in. I got my bat on some more of those balls when they were over the plate, and I also learned how to get the hell out of the way when they weren't.

Rich was always doing crazy things like that, but he taught me to hit. He was one of the first people who worked with me.

People always said I swung too hard. First time I picked up a bat, that's how it was. But that's the way I always swung, right from the start. People like Rich saw that given my size, I needed to generate force, and they saw that I could make contact even when I swung hard.

It's funny, I almost became a catcher, because my brother was one. He went to catching camp and I tagged along. I liked catching, for a while. But I was figuring out what I could do best. Pretty early on, I was going my own way. In Little League, I usually played shortstop, but I pitched, too. I was trying to find the way to play that worked for me, and it was already feeling like shortstop was my natural position.

Even though I had some baseball heroes, that didn't influence me directly in what position I wanted to play, or how I hit. Barry Bonds was the biggest thing in baseball if you were growing up where I did, but I knew I'd find whatever success I would have in baseball in a different way. A guy built like me wasn't going to succeed by trying to be Barry Bonds. But I did love to watch him play.

I wasn't as crazy as the Red Sox fans are by any means, but we definitely watched the San Francisco Giants every single night. At first I didn't follow a particular guy on the Giants. But I loved Barry Bonds after he got there in 1993. I was nine when he arrived, and I thought he was the best player in baseball and the best hitter. At that point in his career he was stealing a lot of bases and playing good defense. There wasn't anything he couldn't do on a baseball field. He was like Superman. That's the way I viewed him, but I didn't want to be him. I played shortstop growing up and he played left field. He was Superman, and I wasn't.

My dad and I would sit there in the living room watching the TV, and when Barry came up we would always be like, "Okay, is he going to hit one out?" Even when I was a little kid it was just fun watching him. He had his bat wiggle and wore that earring. He was what the Giants stood for. He was the best player in the game for the longest time. I was fortunate he was on the team that I loved, so I got a chance to watch him night in and night out.

Baseball wasn't the only thing, either. We were always big sports fans. I followed all the local teams.

For football, I was a huge San Francisco 49ers fan. I always followed them. That was a great run. I was a little kid when Joe Montana, Jerry Rice, Ronnie Lott, and all those guys played. I was lucky to watch that because those were some of the greatest teams of all time.

To see Joe Montana and know his story, I mean, he was an underdog from the time he played in college right up until the time he got to the NFL. There wasn't a person in the world who said, "Joe Montana stinks," or, "I hate Joe Montana." You couldn't hate him. Everybody loved Joe Montana. You could not *not* love him.

Joe Montana was the best and I was fortunate to watch him every Sunday when I was so young. It was the best show in town. He was a winner. He carried himself that way and he proved it on the field.

My other favorite sports team, on the other hand, wasn't a winner back then.

I'm a huge Sacramento Kings fan. The Kings had come to Sacramento from Kansas City in 1985, and my dad had gotten us season tickets. We would go to every single home game and watch them get their asses kicked pretty much each time. I mean, they got the shit beaten out of them. They were 29-53 or 23-59 or 24-58 or whatever for something like five straight years and we would still go to every game. It was the original Arco Arena, which seated eleven thousand, and we would go there when I was about five or six years old. It was when they built the new Arco Arena, which seats seventeen thousand, that they started getting kind of good— around the time I was in high school, so that was huge.

My favorite Kings player of all time was Mitch Richmond. He was on the Kings forever. They called him "the Rock" and he would score something like twenty-five points a night. I never lost my love for the Kings. You have to have your loyalties.

I not only watched every sport I could, I also played every sport I could. I played point guard in the local age-group league every single year all the way up until my freshman year. I played just about anything else that involved competing. That included Ping-Pong. My mom bought me this little half-sized Ping-Pong table when I was a kid and we'd play all the time.

My mom is like me in that she's extremely competitive. I mean, you could be playing nickels with her, and she'd be ready to fight. There was nothing my mom thought she couldn't do, because that's just how she's made.

I would play her in Ping-Pong, and my mom was really good. When I got better and finally began to beat her, she'd be throwing paddles and cursing. She'd be going nuts when she lost. I guess I get a lot of my attitude from my mom.

In junior high, in gym class, we'd play bombardment. It's probably not even allowed anymore, but we had this crazy gym teacher who would have us play it in pretty much every PE class.

Bombardment was kind of like dodgeball. It was a game where they put a bunch of hard volleyballs in the middle of the basketball court and two teams lined up against each wall. The PE teacher would blow the whistle and you had to run up, grab the ball, and go back to this other line without being hit by another ball.

When the whistle blew, you'd go all out to get a ball, then you'd just start throwing them and pegging people. I thought it was awesome to play. I pretty much went kamikaze on everybody. I didn't give a damn. If they were throwing them at me, I'd be dodging them, and if I had a ball in my hand, I was ready to hurt people. Sometimes I could catch a ball, dodge a ball, and unleash another ball at the same time. Winning and unleashing the fury were my main objectives.

I was good at not getting hit. There were times when the PE teacher would set it up where it was five guys against me. And I'd still be kicking everybody's asses.

Seriously, it was a fun game. There were usually the shy girls in the back of the gym, and I remember I let one throw go pretty good one time and it sailed on me and it smoked this girl. I mean, when that ball hit her, she went down hard. She was a friend of mine and I was like, Oh, shit, I just hammered this girl in the head.

She got up then, and she seemed like she would live. She said, "That's all right, Dustin." She knew me, so she got it. Then I just continued to kick ass. It was like playing with no fear and that's how I played baseball. It didn't matter what sport I played when I was growing up because I was going to play as hard as I could in anything. So, I played like that in football, basketball, and even all the other PE sports. There was no point in playing a sport half-assed. That's not what I'm really about. I gave 100 percent in everything I did, even in school. Even in PE class.

2

Break a Leg

My brother finished with Little League the next year, so my dad started coaching me. I was eight years old and I was damned if I was going to be on a team that was 2-20 ever again. And I wasn't. In fact, we didn't lose a single game in the years when I was eight, nine, ten, or eleven. When I was twelve we lost one game, and that was in the City Tournament after going undefeated in the regular season.

We were in the winners' bracket finals in the City Tournament, where it was double elimination. I was pitching. A guy hit a home run off me to win the game, but that was only one loss for us. We were still going to get a chance to come back and play them in the finals.

But my shoulder was aching. It was my first sports injury. I always played so hard, diving around and stuff. I ended up hitting the ground too hard diving for a ball, and when I got up my shoulder was throbbing. My parents took me to the doctor to check it out.

They did the X-rays, and sure enough, it was fractured. I

wouldn't be able to play now, and that sucked bad enough. But then it became clear that the doctor who was examining me thought it was a case of child abuse. Other people were brought in to look at my shoulder. They started interrogating my parents, as if my parents had been the reason my shoulder was injured.

I remember sitting there, a twelve-year-old, and all these people were saying to my parents, "Have you ever abused your child?"

My mom and dad said, "What the heck? Are you kidding me?" It took a while, but finally they were able to explain how I'd been hurt. It was a really strange experience.

I was hurt and couldn't play for a while, even though my team had to play that last game for the City Championship title.

Almost as soon as I was in a sling, I was testing out the shoulder. What I was figuring out was that it really only hurt to throw, not to swing the bat. It was my last year of Little League and we had come so far and I always wanted to win. But I wasn't supposed to play.

That week, my mom went to Las Vegas on a trip. Dad and I went to the game, and he said that since I couldn't play, I could at least be the first-base coach so I could be there with the team.

The game started and I was coaching first base, and I just couldn't stand it, not being in the game.

I kept telling my dad, "Just put me in and let me hit. I can swing. It doesn't hurt my arm at all."

My mom was away, and if she had been there, that would have been the end of it. But I just kept begging to play, and my dad thought about it and said, "Okay . . . I'll put you in for two innings, just so you'll stop bugging me. I'll put you in center field, but you have to promise me not to throw the ball." He wanted me to take anything I caught and run it in.

I played center field for two innings, waiting for my turn to bat. The deal was, I could only play two innings, and then I'd be taken out whether I got to hit or not. We were losing by three runs. I looked at where I was in the batting order, and I wasn't sure I'd even get to the plate before I had to come out.

But when it was my team's turn to hit, guys kept getting on base. We had the bases loaded and suddenly I was up. I swung hard and there it went—a grand slam. We won the game and I was pretty excited. My dad was, too.

But after the game, as we went home, he turned to me as he was driving.

He said, "Man, your mom can't find out about this."

I agreed. It seemed like a simple enough plan. Until in the local paper the next day it said that I had played, and that I had hit a grand slam to win the game.

My mom got home from her trip, and with my parents having already been questioned about abusing me, I thought she was going to kick my dad's ass. But she calmed down pretty quickly. Like I've said, my mom is so competitive, and so is my dad, and it was just one of those things where they knew that this was going to be my life, even though I was so young. They saw that it was just so much fun for me, winning and being a part of that. They understood that not to play in that championship game would have been hard for me to take.

And besides, my shoulder was no worse than it would have been if I hadn't played. So my dad didn't get his ass kicked after all.

My parents just let me have fun. When I was a kid, the house I grew up in had a wooden door that led to the backyard. I hung my glove on the door and would throw a ball at the glove as if I were throwing to first base, over and over, nonstop. The door got worn from all the pounding. When my parents decided to remodel the house, they put in sliding glass doors leading to the yard, so I couldn't do that anymore. Instead I used our big brick fireplace, throwing the ball at the bricks and catching it. My mom and dad let me—they didn't care. But when I cracked four bricks, which then had to be replaced, they started telling me, "Well, don't throw it so hard." But I kept getting bigger, and I was something like twelve years old, and I just kept doing it.

One day, I was throwing a tennis ball against the fireplace and pretending I was turning a double play. I'd fire the ball off the bricks, catch it, then turn and fire it at my mom, who was sitting on the couch. She's such a good athlete, she was having no problem taking my throws and then throwing them right back to me.

But we had this really huge clock on the wall, right above her head. One of the throws went off her hand and hit the clock, shattering the glass and sending it flying everywhere, then knocking the clock right off the wall. The clock came down and hit her on the head and landed on a glass table next to the couch, shattering that, too.

I thought I was going to be in the worst trouble ever. But my mom said, "Don't worry about the clock or the table, we'll get new ones—just keep throwing the ball." She knew how much fun I was having. I think she was also having a lot of fun herself. Later that day, my grandparents came over and they yelled at my mom. "Hey, you need to stop throwing the ball inside the house!" I had the feeling it wasn't the first time they'd told her that.

It was the same thing when football season came around. We'd watch the 49ers on *Monday Night Football* and my dad and I would be playing football in the house. There were always times when I was trying to throw balls or catch balls or something in our living room.

MY BROTHER WAS playing catcher for the baseball team at Shasta College, a community college over in Redding, right by Mount Shasta. That fall, he and some of his teammates got into a league. They were mostly guys from the local junior colleges, including Sacramento City College. Those schools have pretty competitive programs.

Redding was about two hours from Woodland. Every weekend my parents and I would drive up to watch Brett's fall-league games. But one time my brother's team didn't have enough players. Their shortstop had gotten sick, so he didn't show. My brother suggested I play on the team. My equipment bag was always in my parents' car, because sometimes they played two games, and in between games I'd get dressed and go hit or take ground balls.

The other guys took a look at me, this scrawny kid who had just turned thirteen in August, and I think I must have weighed about ninety-five pounds, so they weren't too excited about that idea. But Brett kept saying I was good, and they weren't going to be sorry. "I'm telling you," he said, "my little brother can play."

They said, "He's going to get hurt." Brett just laughed at that.

I played in this junior college fall-league game and I went 4 for 4. Four singles. I was laying out rockets, for the size I was then.

I'd never played on a big, full-sized field before. It was humongous. I led off the game with a line drive up the middle, and then I got to take a lead off first base, which I'd never done before. You couldn't do that in Little League. I came off the base and took a lead, then a little more. But then the pitcher spun around and I dove and I just missed getting picked off. I decided I wouldn't worry about taking leads for now. I was just worried the pitcher was going to hit me with a pitch the next time I got up, for being thirteen and getting a hit off him.

The older guys were like, "Who the hell is this kid?" My brother just kept laughing. Brett was always great about supporting everything I did, and his work ethic got him to junior college ball. I learned a lot from him about working hard but making it enjoyable.

On the way home I was tired, and I could tell that my parents were quietly proud of the way I played. That was the great part of growing up, the way they were there when I had new experiences. It was another long drive from a baseball game, and something to talk about and laugh about. All the good things that happened when I was a kid had something to do with baseball.

THE NEXT SUMMER I continued in the thirteen-year-old level of Senior Little League. I wasn't very strong. I hadn't grown into my body. But I was always good. I played solid defense at shortstop. I always hit for high average but didn't hit many home runs.

As I continued to mature and get older, I developed as a player. Once I got to Woodland High, it was a first step in moving toward what was the biggest thing there, to try to play for the high school varsity.

At the start of ninth grade, I was actually recruited to play football by Mike Pappas, the freshman football coach, who was also the freshman baseball coach.

We always played flag football in PE, and Mike was my PE teacher, too. I played quarterback and threw the ball pretty well. I didn't throw it exactly sidearm, but I threw it a little down angle, so I was able to get it over the line.

He asked me, "Hey, did you ever think about playing football?"

I said, "No, not really. I play baseball and that's my main sport."

He said, "Why don't you come out and play?"

I said, "I weigh a hundred and ten pounds. This doesn't seem like a good idea."

"No, you'll do fine," he said. "Listen, we'll play you at quarterback. All you have to do is, we'll put you in the shotgun if you're going to pass, and we'll run an option here and there. You're pretty fast so you won't get hit."

I said, "All right, that sounds good, not getting hit . . ."

"Then you'll play . . . ?"

I said, "Well, I have to ask my parents." It was one of those things.

Next, the coach came over to our house. He only lived a couple of blocks away from us.

He convinced my parents that he would take care of me. He told them that the team would run the ball a lot more that year, and that I wouldn't get hit much.

Once we started playing, we actually *passed* the ball a lot more, and most of the offense went through me. I was running around and throwing the ball. So I guess the probability of getting hurt was a lot higher than he'd told my parents, because he had made it sound as if I would take the snap and just hand it off to a running back.

But it was fun, because I learned a lot about myself playing football. When you put the pads on, yeah, you could be small, but you could still go up there and thump somebody. I think that's when my mentality changed. I was hitting guys like I was 170 pounds and not 110 pounds.

So just like that, I was playing quarterback. And it was a pretty interesting experience. All my friends—Woodland's a small town—played on the team. And once we got going, I was actually pretty good. It was fun, too. I wasn't the biggest guy, that was for sure, but I competed. I didn't have a lot of arm strength, so I threw with that semi-sidearm. It was kind of weird looking.

Everything went well until the eighth game of the season. I think we were something like 5-2, and we were playing Elk Grove, the best team in the Sacramento area at that time. The varsity at Elk Grove had Lance Briggs on their team, who now plays for the Bears. They've put four guys into the NFL. They are intense about their football.

We came out and we were beating them. And right before the half, we ran a play and some huge kid hit me and shattered my whole leg.

I was down on the ground and I thought it was a cramp. But my first instinct was, This is the worst pain I've ever felt. But maybe I can play in the second half.

They helped me to the sidelines. They couldn't see how bad it was. It was a cold day, and I was wearing two pairs of socks. They pulled down my socks and my leg looked like it was the size of a basketball. Bones were shattered. It was awful.

They rushed me to the doctor and during that thirty-minute ambulance ride the only thing I kept thinking was, I'll never be able to play baseball again.

That was my life. That's all I did. That's all I ever wanted to do. I was playing football just because my baseball coach had told me it would be fun. And now I had gone and possibly messed up the whole baseball thing.

I ended up having surgery right away. I was in a cast for a while, then I was hobbling around all through the winter and spring. I ended up missing, with rehab and everything, the first six games of my freshman baseball season. I was out six months and ended up playing baseball, but it was really limited. I would play five innings and then they would take me out because my leg would start throbbing.

At that age, you could play Babe Ruth League and all kinds of stuff like that, but high school freshman baseball was when you started to see if you could do it for real. If I could eventually get to the varsity team, I could play for a college scholarship, and that had always been my biggest goal.

Looking back, that football injury was an important event because it set my mind on one thing—baseball. It was the first time there had ever been a chance something I cared so much about could be taken away from me. With the possibility that baseball success might have been all over with that injury, I wanted it that much more.

It was then that I decided that baseball was what I wanted to do for the rest of my life.

Rob Rinaldi

Former Baseball Coach

Woodland High School

When Dustin was going through school, Woodland High was tenth, eleventh, and twelfth grades.

I had coached his older brother at the high school, and I knew the Pedroia family pretty well and had spent some time at their home. Even at Little League age, Dustin would come out to our practices and work out with the varsity baseball team on occasion.

So I knew him before he got to the high school. Obviously, he had a lot going for him athletically, and when he was eleven and twelve years old and he'd practice with the team, he'd get very upset with me if I took even a little bit off my throws when I was pitching to him in batting practice, or took a little off my swings when I was hitting ground balls for fielding practice. He'd start yelling, "Stop doing that, Coach! I want you to give me your best stuff!"

A lot of what you see in him now, he already had way back then, including him talking smack to the varsity kids, who were friends of his brother's. Woodland is a small town, so they all knew each other. Dustin was always talking.

In ninth grade, Dustin had broken his leg playing football at the middle school. He had not been able to play much baseball in ninth grade. I saw him play later that year, and he wasn't moving too well.

By the time I got him that next summer, between his ninth- and tenth-grade years, he'd recovered from the injury. We had a summer team. What we would do was, we would take next year's varsity players and put together a summer team. That year's graduating seniors would go off to play American Legion ball, and we'd get the juniors moving to senior year, the sophomores coming up from the junior varsity, and the occasional freshman who might possibly have a chance to make the team. We'd put them together and we'd go play a bunch of tournaments in the summer.

Dustin was tiny. He couldn't have weighed more than 120 pounds, and he hadn't played much freshman baseball at the junior high school.

And that summer, we had a good group of players, particularly in the middle infield positions. We had a real good senior shortstop, and we had a couple of junior shortstops. It was very competitive for those positions.

It took maybe two games in the summer league for me to say, "He's our shortstop. Everybody else is going to have to move around." From that point on, he played every game. And right off, as a kid who was not even a sophomore yet, he was a leader. We would put him in a game, and everything would solidify around him. He was our best player.

His sophomore year on, the whole defense ran through him.

He was a coach on the field, and when he was batting he brought that confidence and swagger the kids fed off of. His sophomore year was the year we no-hit three teams in a row. Three consecutive games, with five pitchers involved. And later, we lost a no-hitter, 1 to 0.

As a sophomore, Dustin was tiny. But he had it together, and his junior year was better. He hit .448 and was named to the underclassman all-state team. As a junior he hit .459 and was all-league, all-metro, and all-state.

Defensively, he won so many games, not just by making plays in the field but by knowing how to play certain situations, and making the team so much better at doing that.

He was a phenomenal player from day one as a sophomore. He never slowed down. He just kept getting physically stronger. And he just kept getting more confident, if you can even imagine that.

3

Rising Star

I ended up playing ball the summer before my tenth-grade year with a team that was mainly guys from the varsity team. I started getting back into it after my injury. I always had the hand-eye coordination, so I was fine there, but because of the damage of that injury my legs had never gotten stronger. I was slower, too. Before I'd broken my leg I'd been pretty fast—not fast like some guys, but fast for me.

I tried out for the varsity my sophomore year. There had been, I think, only two other guys to make the varsity as a sophomore in my hometown. One of them ended up a first-round pick, Tony Torcato, who played with the Giants a few years back, and the other was Mike Griffin, who pitched for five major-league teams, including the Cubs and Yankees, and who later was a pitching coach in the Red Sox minor-league system.

My biggest thing was I wanted to be a shortstop and my sophomore year I ended up making the team. Not only did I make the team, but I ended up leading the team in pretty much every category. That was something I don't think anybody expected. Baseball in that area is big. It's like Texas football, Florida football, and even California football. The high schools hold camps and pretty much everyone goes to them. You are brought up wanting to play high school baseball there. For me to do so well, so young, surprised everybody.

Our team that year was just a bunch of scrappy players. We didn't have anybody out of the ordinary, except me, at that time, I guess. But nobody knew that, because I was a sophomore, weighing 120 pounds at the most.

It was a good bunch of guys and the only thing we cared about was winning and we all loved each other. It was like family. The guys I grew up with my whole life were all playing together on the varsity. One best friend was playing second base. My other best friend was playing third. A bunch of pitchers were all my buddies. It was like we were fielding a team from our cul-de-sac, like we were still just playing a Wiffle ball game, but now it was the Woodland High School team.

It was just fun. It's not like you couldn't yell at someone for screwing up, because they were just like family. That's why I think I play the way I do. I started playing with a passion at a young age. Everyone was holding each other responsible for the way they played the game. We were crushing each other, because we were friends. There wasn't one thing I couldn't say to another guy, and there wasn't one thing he couldn't say to me. We were all friends and we all wanted to win. I think our high school coach had something to do with that. He taught us how to win. We played in one of the toughest divisions in California.

There were always really good players in that league, and our team was always good. I think it was because of our mentality and our closeness.

WE WENT TO the section finals that year and played Fairfield. I remember in the section final game I was 4 for 4, and I came up to bat with our team down one run in the last inning—and I struck out. I felt like I had let everybody down. I felt like Chris Webber—remember that time he called that timeout in the Final Four for Michigan in 1993, when they had no timeouts left, and it cost them the title? That was how it felt to strike out. I was like, "Damn!" And it was going to be all year before I could make up for it.

I kept playing, and practicing, and getting ready to go. I waited through the winter, wanting the season to begin.

But the next year, my junior year, I started to get noticed.

Our high school team played tough. Woodland's a farm town, and people work hard, and it breeds a certain attitude. We've probably only had two guys who were even six feet tall, but everybody played aggressively, often against bigger teams. We'd try to break up the double play when nobody did that, because it was kind of illegal. You're not supposed to slide past the base, and we were straight-up going after people. Our team, because we weren't very big, always figured we were going to outwork the other team. That's how we won and that's how we all got our work ethic.

Our pitchers were throwing at guys when they had to. If some guy was 2 for 2, our pitchers were buzzing the tower. We were playing baseball and it was fun. We went up there to compete and put some hurt on those guys and then my junior year came, and I had another great season. I hit .459.

That summer, an area scout with the Giants, the late Doug McMillan, invited me to something called the 2000 Area Code Games, which was a tournament in Long Beach for the best amateur players around, set up in these all-star teams grouped by area code. All the scouts were going to be there and this was where *Baseball America* got its Top 100 Prospects.

There was actually a tryout game first, near home. I was nervous, man. In the Area Code Games, they were using wood bats, and I'd never swung a wood bat in my life, except when I would pick one up at the Big 5 Sporting Goods by my house.

I was so excited. We went into this sports store to get a wood bat. I didn't even know what to get.

I saw a rack of Mizuno bats and I knew major leaguers were using them. Mike Piazza used one, so I thought, This is going to work out pretty good.

I grabbed the bat and it felt good. I remember it was thirty-two inches long, and weighed twenty-nine ounces. It was basically the smallest bat ever. Everyone was laughing at me. People were saying, "Why are you swinging that?"

"Dude, I'm a hundred and twenty pounds. This is all I *got*."

I remember the first pitch I saw at the tryout. I was fortunate because the tryout was at my high school. That was a big advantage because this was my town. We have an armory in the back over the left-field wall, and that first pitch came at me and I got a hold of it. The ball hit the middle of the armory on the fly. It was just a rocket line drive.

I remember running around the bases and thinking, If these are the best players in Northern California, I'm going to kick all their asses.

I was a little different then than I am now, but I still remember thinking that. I got another hit in the game and ended up making the team and going down to Long Beach.

We went down to the Area Code Games a week after the try-out and I played. The first game I went 3 for 3 and started playing really well. Still, you see all the college coaches there but because of recruiting rules they can't talk to you until a month later. I didn't know what to expect.

I was thinking to myself, At least one guy will say "Hey Dustin, how you doing?" But there was nothing.

I was kind of pissed because you read about all these other guys who were playing. There was a guy who had come all the way from Georgia, and everybody was watching him. And I'm thinking, He's not 3 for 3 in the game. He's not helping his team win. How come they're mentioning him and not me?

I was named to the tournament All-Star Team, but nobody seemed to be paying attention.

That made me think, If they're not mentioning me, then I have to do something different to become a better player.

I didn't know that much about how colleges recruited, and I didn't know what to expect. Because there had seemed to be a lack of interest in me at the Area Code Games, I was wondering how that process was going to go. I kept thinking, I've played well . . . somebody has to notice that. But it was also becoming clearer that my size was a factor. I wasn't looking like I was going to suddenly shoot up to six feet, two inches. But in my mind, why did that matter? If I could play, I could play.

From July 1 before senior year, colleges can start calling your house or visiting in person. I remember it was six in the morning when I got my first phone call. It was local—Sacramento State. I was like, "Sac State sucks." They didn't win that many games back then. I didn't want to go there and lose. Yeah, it would be awesome to get a scholarship and all, but Sac State?

The other reason I wasn't too big on Sac State was that the guy who called me had been a coach at a rival high school. He had just left to go to Sac State and at his high school he used to have his pitchers throw at me all the time. So I was pissed and I said, "I don't want to talk to you. Screw you. You guys threw at me."

That was my first call at six in the morning.

I had to go over to school that day. When I got back home, my next call was from Arizona State and it was the recruiting coordinator, Jay Sferra, who said, "You know, Dustin, we are very interested in you. Are you doing anything tonight at seven o'clock?"

I said, "Probably going to hit, or something. What's the deal?"

He said, "I'm going to fly in and I want to meet with you and your family to go over some things."

"Sweet!"

As that first recruiting day went on, the phone kept ringing. I ended up getting sixty-five phone calls on day one.

It was one of those times I was kind of overwhelmed. My whole life, the only thing I wanted was to go to college, play college baseball, and get a scholarship. That day, it was one of those deals where I could go anywhere I wanted to. And I had never had that luxury in my life.

I always played to win and I couldn't care less what people thought of me.

I ended up talking with everybody and I was very respectful on the phone, except to the Sac State guy. I was excited and you could probably tell, hearing my voice. I'm sure every coach who called me thought I was going there because I was so excited about it.

Seven o'clock came and the Arizona State recruiting coach showed up at my house. My mom cooked him dinner. She was sort of going crazy, talking away. My dad, when he gets excited, gets quiet and doesn't know what to say.

I had lucked out because my uncle Phil Snow, the football coach, had moved from Cal Berkeley to Arizona State in 1992 and was the defensive coordinator there. He'd kept telling Coach Sferra and Coach Pat Murphy, the head baseball coach, "Hey, guys, you need to check out my nephew. He's awesome."

Coach Murphy said, "Well, how big is he?"

My uncle said, "He's five foot seven, one hundred and thirty pounds."

Coach Murphy said, "Well, we really don't need a batboy. That's just ridiculous, Phil."

"No," my uncle said, "I'm telling you—he can hit home runs, he steals bases, he plays shortstop, and he's awesome."

Based on that conversation, Coach Murphy had decided to have a recruiter take a look at me.

At that time, besides coaching Arizona State in their 2000 season, Coach Murphy was coaching the Netherlands baseball team for the 2000 Olympics, in Sydney, Australia. Because of that, he'd never really gotten a chance to see me play in person.

But I had been playing with the Northern California team in a tournament in Peoria, outside Phoenix, and while I didn't know it at the time, Coach Sferra had come out to see me play. A coach named Rob Bruno had this team out of Nor Cal and he invited all the best players from our part of the state to play in these two- or three-day tournaments. They're called "showcase tournaments," and I said, "Yeah, maybe I'll give it a chance."

When I'd heard there was a tournament in Arizona, I really went so I could see my uncle and his family, because I hadn't seen them in a while. I went down there to play and Jay Sferra was in the stands. I think Coach Sferra was there mainly because my uncle kept telling him, "My nephew can play."

Everyone was saying, "Yeah, you're just bragging about him."

But once Coach Sferra saw me and the way I played, it reminded him of the kind of baseball he liked. Coach Sferra played the game and he's a hard-nosed guy. He loves Lenny Dykstra, who had played for the Mets and Phillies and was known as "Nails." I think he saw the way I played, and I think he liked it.

He said later that I was the best high school baseball player he'd seen—not the best athlete, but the best baseball player.

What Coach Murphy later told me was that Coach Sferra said to him, "Murph, this guy, I'm telling you, we're not going to have to worry about shortstop for the next four years."

When they told me that, I wondered if what he meant was four years because they didn't think I had a chance of getting drafted. But when Coach Sferra came to the house on his recruiting visit, he told my parents he could definitely see me becoming a major-league second baseman.

"You mean shortstop," my mother said.

So, the home visit went great, but during the whole evening there was no discussion of scholarship money. But this was the school I wanted to play for, and I was ready to get it done.

I felt that Arizona State was my top choice because my uncle was there, which made it a little more comfortable, and I also wanted to go there because my dad always told me that if I ever had the opportunity to play college baseball, Arizona State was the ultimate. Barry Bonds went there. Reggie Jackson went there. My dad said, "When you think of college baseball, you think about Arizona State—without a doubt."

I wanted Arizona State. That was all there was to it. I was getting recruited by Miami, Texas, Florida; they were all calling me. Tulane offered me a five-year scholarship the first day. I said to myself, "Five years? Shit. It might end up being ten because I'm not the smartest guy."

The dinner with the Arizona State coach went great, and later they called to say they wanted me to take a recruiting trip to Tempe. Actually, the recruiting trip was going to be a month later, because Coach Murphy was flying back, and because he and his wife were having a baby, their son Kai, he was only going to be in town for three days.

There were three other players going to visit Arizona State from the Sacramento area, who were all really good. They were all pitchers: J. P. Howell, Nick Thomas, and Chris Kinsey. They were all in my league, so I had played against them. If I played against you at that time, I hated you. I was ready to fight them.

I had already planned all my recruiting trips and in a month's time I was going to go to Arizona State, Long Beach State, Florida, Texas, and Miami. Those were going to be my five trips. We had them all set.

If I was going to play college baseball, I was going to win. I wasn't interested in doing anything else and those five programs were the top five.

So I went on my trip to Arizona State. It turned out that J. P., Nick, and Chris were good guys. We all got along. Then I sat down with Coach Murphy. He's huge. He was a boxer. He said later he looked at me and wondered what he was going to do with a college ballplayer who had a sixth-grade body.

WHEN IT CAME to the meeting where it was time to hear the scholarship offer, both my parents came. We all loved the campus and the baseball tradition at ASU. Everything was first class, too. They took care of us.

We went into that final meeting and what I expected was that it was a matter of them just giving me the full scholarship. But Coach Murphy said, "Okay, we're going to offer you tuition."

That was something like 45 percent of the total cost of attending. I was kind of staring at Coach Murphy and he said, "Well, what do you think about that, Dustin?"

I said, "Well, Coach, I have full rides to Miami, Texas, Long Beach State, and I even have a five-year offer from a school that I'm not even taking a trip to—and that school, Tulane, just went to the College World Series. I'm not a businessman yet, I'm a baseball player, and I only care about one thing—that's winning."

Coach Murphy was looking at me, listening.

"Financially, my parents are fortunate enough," I told him. "My dad put himself through hell, working his butt off, so that financially we could afford any school we wanted. But I'm not going to spend his money just because you know my uncle, or because you know my dad has some money."

Coach Murphy said, "Well, Dustin, we're going to win with you or without you."

I was trying to stay calm.

I said, "I'll guarantee you this: if I don't come to ASU, you won't win as many games as if I do come here."

I was seventeen years old and I was telling this to the most successful college baseball coach there was, a guy who two years before had been national Coach of the Year.

He looked at me and just smiled, and shook his head like he was thinking, I'm really wanting to kick your ass right now.

I remember right when I said that, my mother turned to me and said, "Dustin! *Stop!*"

I said, "Well, it's true."

You know what? I meant it. It was from my heart. I believed in every word I was saying. I completely understand what Coach Murphy was thinking, looking at me then. And I knew he only had so many scholarships he could give out, and that there were a lot of good players who wanted to come to Arizona State. But I also knew I could prove him wrong.

A week went by, and my dad wanted me to go back down to ASU for another visit. For my dad, that was first and foremost, to get back in front of Coach Murphy and talk it over face-to-face. I let a week go by, but then Coach Murphy called and gave me a negotiating deadline, like we were talking contract: "Hey, we need to know by Saturday; otherwise we're going to take your scholarship off the table."

My parents and I talked it over. I told my dad, "Hey, if they don't come up with a full scholarship, I'm going somewhere else. Why don't you tell Coach Murphy that!"

The next day, I got home from school, and Dad was smiling. Coach Murphy had called my dad and said, "All right, we're offering him whatever he wants. We want him to be a Sun Devil."

I called him right back up and I said, "All right, I'm committing to you right now. I want to go to Arizona State and be a part of this program."

That's how that process got done.

Ron McNutt

Coach, Carson Capitols

Carson City, Nevada

My wife, Terrie, and I founded the Capitols in 1978. It was an extensive travel team for twenty-three years. We had athletes from all over the country come to play in Carson City, Nevada. We played a schedule of sixty to eighty games each summer. This is part of what attracted top players.

The teams consisted of mostly senior graduates with some college freshmen and a few high school underclassmen. Many times college and professional scouts would recommend our program to prospective players or would tell me about a player that I should extend an invitation to come to Carson City to. I had heard about Dustin from quite a few scouts and college coaches. His high school coach, Rob Rinaldi, had contacted me regarding Dustin.

Many of the Capitols went on to play in the major leagues. Matt Williams, who had a great career with the Giants and Diamondbacks; Donovan Osborne of the Cardinals; Darrell Rasner, who was with the Yankees last year; J. P. Howell of the Tampa Bay Rays; Charlie Kerfeld, who played for the Houston Astros; and Bobby Ayrault with the Philadelphia Phillies are among those who spent their summers playing for the Capitols. And sixteen of Dustin's teammates went on to play Division I college baseball.

Our clubhouse was unique. We had an old railroad boxcar. It came to Reno via Sacramento, where they have a train graveyard. We had the wheels torched off in Reno and then put it on a flat-bed truck down to Carson City to be laid on a concrete slab. The Carson High shop classes built some nice lockers and local companies donated materials. It was very upscale with tile, carpet, stereo, and couches. It was their clubhouse.

The Capitols were affiliated with several organizations over the years, such as the American Legion, Connie Mack, and the Continental Amateur Baseball Association, to name a few. The benefit of playing in more than forty states was the exposure and top-notch competition for the players. We always traveled in luxury motor coaches with card tables, televisions, and VCRs. We took the airlines when it was long distance and again gave them the feeling of a professional environment where the whole commitment was to baseball.

Some of the players stayed with families in town who hosted them, and some with other players who lived nearby. Our town regarded the Capitols as a minor-league or rookie-league team.

When Dustin came to us, he was a very enthusiastic, energetic kid. He was very well liked and quickly became the team leader. He was determined to do well, and he loved the game. He wanted to play the game, and he wanted to talk about the game when he wasn't playing. There have been very few players who've gone through the Capitols program, even though so many of them have gone on and done well, who had Dustin's desire. He had the mannerisms, work ethic, and attitude of being very professional, even at that young age. He was one of those rare players who you could see would go to higher levels not just because of his ability, but because of the way he went about things. He had heart and obvious determination. He was a winner. He was also dedicated to his family. They were his positive support and encouragement and also spent the summer watching Dustin play for the Capitols wherever the games took us.

Being on the Capitols gave him a great opportunity to prepare for Arizona State.

Dustin was the leading hitter at .432. Because of his outstanding ability to play the middle infield, he was always a topic of conversation among observing coaches and scouts.

On the lighter side, Dustin was a chatterbox. In the dugout, in the locker room, on the bus, he was always chattering. I think he must have chattered all night in his sleep. He always had a good time. He enjoyed the camaraderie of his teammates. Our second baseman, Joe Hooft (University of Miami, Arizona State, Texas Rangers), once told Dustin that he was the best shortstop he had ever seen. Dustin replied, "I would say the same to you about second basemen, but I've already played there." That's Dustin! But when he stepped between the lines, it was showtime.

4

The Carson City Kid

Senior year, playing for Coach Matt Bryson, we ended up in the sectional playoffs, playing Jesuit High from Carmichael, California. J. P. Howell, who is playing these days for the Tampa Bay Rays, ended up beating us. He threw the ball extremely well and we got beat pretty good.

But I hadn't struck out. In fact, I hadn't struck out all season.

I didn't know that, to be honest. I only found out after the last game of the year. I'm not big into looking at numbers and stuff like that, especially in high school. I was just playing the game and having fun and playing to win. That's all I cared about. I remember one of my teammates came up to me and said, "Hey, do you know you didn't strike out once this year?"

I said, "No, man. I had to have struck out a few times."

He said, "Dude, you didn't strike out one time."

I started thinking about it. I tried to think about all the good pitchers we faced all year and I'm thinking, He didn't strike me out, and that guy didn't strike me out, either.

That was pretty cool, but I didn't read too much into it. I was just playing and having fun; but it was quite an accomplishment.

And someone was paying attention to me: I got invited that summer after high school to play in Carson City, for a travel team called the Carson Capitols. That was a big honor in that area. J. P. ended up playing for them, too. That summer, they played a sixty-game schedule in a sixty-day season. It was kind of like professional baseball. You played every day.

Carson City is 150 miles away from Woodland. I was seventeen years old. I'd started young for my grade because I have an August birthday. I wasn't sure how my parents would feel about me being away at that age. I told my dad and he said, "You have to go do it. You'll get a lot better. You'll play sixty games."

I lived in a place called the Nugget Casino. The coach, Ron McNutt, kind of set it up for me. Ron was the varsity coach at Carson High, and he had set up this summer team to get his best guys good competition. Guys also came from all over Nevada and Northern California to play for the Capitols. We'd play teams from all over the country, and travel to tournaments. I went up there and got my room at the Nugget. It was pretty much a hundred bucks a month of living expenses and they had a big buffet in the morning down in the dining room. It was one of those things where I just needed a place to sleep. In Carson City that summer, I spent just about all my time, other than sleeping, at the field—as I still do today. That's where I got my routine: at a young age, playing for the Capitols. I would wake up and go downstairs to eat. It was a $2.99 breakfast, which was awesome. You know the casinos, they want the gamblers who've been up all night to have an excuse not to go home, to get a little food in them so they can just keep going.

The Gambler's Special had eggs and bacon and whatever else

there was. I kept going in there every single day because we played a lot of home games and we didn't travel that much, which was kind of a cool deal. The waitresses at the Nugget got to know me because I pretty much sat at the same table and ordered the same thing every day. I'm a big routine guy and have always liked to do basically the same thing every day, and was that way even at that age, which is kind of weird. I would finish my breakfast and just head to the field.

The Capitols played at the field at Carson High, which was named Ron McNutt Field, after our coach. It had an actual clubhouse there, and it was a first-class setup. It was something I wasn't used to, because at my high school, if you needed to change, you would walk around the corner and change your shirt really quick so no one would see you.

In Carson City we had a locker room with televisions in it. I had never been a part of anything like that, so I thought it was the coolest thing in the world to have food in your locker room and stuff like that. I hung out there in the clubhouse all day long, until the game started that night.

I wasn't going to school in the summer and so it was as if I were playing minor-league baseball. It felt professional. I told myself that I was, hopefully, getting ready for an opportunity to do what I wanted to do.

That's where I think I got my routine. To this day I get to the park at one o'clock for a major-league night game, and that's pretty early. A lot of guys don't get there nearly that early, but I just enjoy getting to the field because I love playing baseball.

Carson City was where I figured out that I wanted baseball to be my full-time job.

It was kind of crazy. My parents would drive me there and my mom would sometimes stay with me. It was summertime and she would stay with me a couple of days and then my dad would come up for a few days. I was young, so it wasn't like they were totally comfortable leaving me on my own, living in a casino. I wasn't wild or anything, but I did like to have fun.

They were always there, driving back and forth from Woodland to see me play. For them to do that for me was unbelievable, given all the demands at the tire stores. That just shows what type of people they were and how dedicated they were to helping me get better.

I played there that whole summer—all sixty games. I played really well. The elevation is nearly five thousand feet, so in that thinner air, all of a sudden I started hitting some home runs. I was still only about 130 pounds. But I started pounding some home runs and I started feeling good about myself. I hit seventeen that summer, and finished with a .432 batting average, the best on the team.

I felt that after my experience with the Capitols, I was getting confident as a player. And that was good, because I'd had a real disappointment just before I went to Carson City.

AT THE END of my senior year, I was really hoping to get drafted. That was obviously a goal, and any time you can get drafted, it's giving you some proof that you may have some potential to move up to professional baseball.

I also felt like I'd done what I needed to do to earn that proof. I'd had another great season my senior year at Woodland High. I had hit .445 and was named Player of the Year for the Sacramento area. I'd been league MVP and all-state. I was feeling that I'd done what it took to show people I had the ability to succeed. I was still only about five feet, five inches tall. But I was playing as well as anybody, I thought.

Then I didn't get drafted. I didn't really even get contacted, not by any team. Not even a couple of letters or anything. It all just rolled by, and I wasn't part of it. After all my successes in high school, nobody wanted to even take a chance on me. I was thinking, Oh, shit. This really sucks.

I felt that more than anything else, it had to do with my size. I had played well enough that that had to be the reason, that I wasn't six foot four. No one believed I'd ever have the body to play major-league baseball. While the scholarship offers had shown that people believed I could be a good college shortstop, no one must have seriously thought I could play in the big leagues. It was kind of a shock, but it didn't change my goal. I wanted to make baseball my work, and I was just going to have to prove everyone wrong.

The 2001 Major League Baseball draft had fifty rounds. There were 1,485 guys drafted, and I wasn't one of them. My team, the San Francisco Giants, had fifty-two picks in that draft and even though I was a guy right in their backyard, they had no interest. That hurt.

And of those 1,485 guys drafted, the first pick of all was a high school kid from Cretin–Derham Hall high school in St. Paul, Minnesota, picked by the team in his backyard, the Twins. He was a catcher, a six-foot-four catcher. His name was Joe Mauer.

Pat Murphy

Head Baseball Coach

Arizona State University

We had recruited Dustin to be our starting shortstop. We heard a lot about him, that he was a gamer. But the questions everyone in college baseball was asking about him were, Is he big enough? Is he strong enough? Will he have the arm to make the throw? We all wondered if he would be physically strong enough to play at this high a level and put up with the demands.

My assistant coach Jay Sferra deserves the credit for seeing what the kid had. Jay was the first one I heard of who said, "No doubt." No doubt he could play, and no doubt Arizona State wouldn't have to worry about who was playing shortstop for us for the next few years.

"This kid is a great one—no doubt," is what Jay said. I took his word for it, even though I'd never seen Dustin play.

Unlike Division I college football programs that can give out eighty-five full scholarships, or basketball, where you have thirteen full scholarships to give to a roster of fourteen or fifteen players, the NCAA limits Division I baseball programs to 11.7 scholarships, which can be broken up into parts.

Usually, if you offer a recruit a scholarship covering tuition, fees, and books, it's a pretty good chunk, even if they're paying room and board. For an out-of-state kid, that's 65 or 70 percent of the scholarship cost. At first that's what we offered, but he kept getting full scholarship offers from other schools and he wanted it from us. So I said to Jay, "If you believe he's that good, let's offer the full scholarship to get this done."

So Dustin was coming in with high expectations on him.

When I first saw this recruit on campus, I was sitting at my desk and he comes walking into my office.

I looked at him and said to myself, "Holy shit . . . This is him?"

He had on a white T-shirt with the sleeves cut off. His arms were skinny and as white as Minnesota in the winter. He flexed his biceps and said, "Hey, how do you like these guns?"

I was thinking, "I hope you can at least field, or your ass will be out of here."

From then on, it wasn't hard to see why he would do well. He walked around with confidence, energy, and a chip on his shoulder. He had spunk that you just didn't see every day. He wanted to be challenged.

His first year I used to go out and take ground balls with him at shortstop. I'm not the most agile person but I can talk a good game. I'd stand out there and talk mad nonsense at him about how he wasn't up to it. I ran a lot of guys off their positions, but he was about the only one to stand up to me. He'd say, "Come on, Coach, I'm way better than you. You're the one who sucks." We'd go at each other, back and forth.

I'd watch him field ground balls and it wasn't very orthodox, but every ball ended up in the glove. And he could throw strikes. That's the most underrated part of his game: he catches everything and he throws strikes. You can't tell me this kid can't play shortstop at any level, including the big leagues.

The first game I saw him play in college, whoever it was we played against, he hit a line drive right to the third baseman. When the guy caught it, Pedro was like, "You've got to be kidding me!"

He ran by the pitcher on the mound and said, "Get ready for that, all day! I'm going to be hitting lasers off you all day."

I yelled at him: "Pedroia, what did you say to him?"

He told me, then he said, "Coach, this guy sucks. We're going to kill him."

We beat them, but the point of it was seeing that this was Pedro. This was him. You know, "We're going to kick your ass." That was his way of doing things. He set the tone. It wasn't like our program sucked and we needed that; he just set the tone.

We've been in the Top Ten, I think, four out of the six years since he's been gone. His presence on this team had a lot to do with that.

In 2005, in what would have been Pedro's senior year, we went to the College World Series. I wore "Pedroia" on my cap during the CWS that year.

We finished third in the country and played about five games in the World Series. After every game, I would get calls from people who saw his name on my cap, asking, "Did something happen to Pedroia?"

I told them he was fine. He was playing in the minor leagues at that point. I told them I put his name on my hat because he deserved to be there. The work he did for the program beforehand is what got us there. He deserved to be there with us in some way.

The kid is going to give you an honest day's work every year. What he does is he makes your team better. Baseball is such a team game and he makes your team better because every time you pitch to this kid—five foot five or whatever he is—you have to bust your ass to get him out, and it ain't easy. He's going to fight you hard, and just when you think you've got him beat, he comes up with something to keep himself alive and eventually beats you.

It's still a team game, but he made the other kids on his team better. It's not just what he says. Half of what he says you don't even listen to. It doesn't matter. It's what he does and who he is.

He is part of the great lore of our great history. He's one of those characters.

Last year, I took a trip to Hawaii with a group of twenty-five friends, family, and former players. People like Andre Ethier (who's with the Dodgers now), Dustin, Willie Bloomquist (now with the Royals), Kevin Tillman (Pat's brother), assistant coaches Josh Holliday and Andy Stankiewicz, and their families. My only requirement was to eat dinner together every night as a group. Anytime we talked baseball or hitting, Pedro would say, "Hey, man. I just see it and hit it."

We would get all technical and everything, and he would just say, "I just see it and hit it. I don't care how."

When he signed his most recent contract, he said to me right out, "I don't care if I can get more money someplace else. I know I can get a better deal. I don't care what anybody says. I'm going to play good every year. It's not going to be the last time I get a contract."

It's just the way he lives his life, and it's true. He just loves competing. He loves being out there. As soon as he realized, "Hey, I'm good enough to do this," it was on.

But when he came in as a freshman, he was a skinny kid who we expected to work hard for his spot, just like everybody else.

We don't promise positions to players when they come in—they have to earn them. He was playing for a position, and we could see that what he responded to most was a challenge, or an obstacle.

We learned that if we told this kid he couldn't do it, he was going to go ahead and show us that he could.

5

Sun Devil

I went to Arizona State that fall of 2001, ready to prove a lot of people wrong. But some things were already changing.

After I had committed there, my uncle got fired. Phil had been an assistant coach with Bruce Snyder, first at Cal and then ASU. After Snyder took ASU to the Rose Bowl in 1996 with an 11-1 record, the next few years weren't as good. After 6-6 seasons in 1999 and 2000, Snyder was fired and everybody on his staff was let go. Phil had left right before I arrived, and joined the coaching staff at the University of California at Los Angeles.

Part of the reason I'd gotten noticed by ASU was my uncle, and part of the reason I had committed to them was because I'd have family nearby. Now Phil wasn't there. That was kind of tough, because I'd felt a little more confident knowing he was my fallback. I had figured that if I needed something, or got a little homesick, I could just go to my uncle's house and hang out and see family.

I was in a new state by myself. It felt isolated. The thing is, it had always been when I was playing a sport, and if I had a bad day, there was someone to talk to—my parents or my friends. Now I had no one to talk to except my teammates. And at that time, we were all trying to make the team. So really, they didn't care if I did badly.

The Arizona State campus is a huge place. At the time there were something like sixty thousand students (it's even larger now), bigger than the whole town of Woodland. And the academics were going to be a lot harder than at Woodland High.

When I got there for my freshman year, I walked into Murph's office wearing a tank top, showing off my skinny arms, and told him, "Start hitting me ground balls."

He looked at me and said, "Who the hell are you?"

I wasn't sure if he was joking or not. It seemed like he'd forgotten who I was.

I said, "I'm your new shortstop."

He said, "Which one are you again?"

I asked, "Why, how many shortstops do you have coming in?"

"Eight," he said.

I thought, Shit. I'm in trouble.

I flexed my biceps and said, "But Coach, check out these guns."

He told me I had no business wearing a cut-off T-shirt.

I got to work showing Murph what I could do. I took ground balls every day. I had a tough time in the beginning. We started fall ball right away and I had to get used to a faster infield, because in the Sacramento area I played on thick grass, kind of like Boston, where you have longer grass with heavy dirt and it rains a lot.

You get to Arizona State and it's like playing on concrete. You're getting missiles coming through the infield. I had a lot of trouble fielding the ball at first. We played, I think, seventeen games in the fall and I made twenty-five errors. But my bat was good. I hit something like .470. I was still raking.

Coach Murphy was really hard on me. There wasn't a day that went by when he wasn't all over me. We would have team meetings every day and he would call me out personally.

He wasn't attacking me for the sake of doing it. I know that now. He was trying to get the most out of me. It just didn't feel like that. I was calling my parents, saying, "The coach hates me and I need to get out of here."

My dad kept telling me, "Hey, you made this commitment and there's no turning back. You have to own up to your responsibilities. You're a man now. You have to figure it out on your own."

The coaches roomed me with Dennis Wyrick, who was the shortstop the previous two years. He had gotten a lot bigger. Now he was six foot three and he was growing out of shortstop, so they were going to move him to third base. To make room for me, supposedly—or for one of the other seven shortstops they brought in.

Dennis was a calming influence. I would go home after a game when I had gone 3 for 3 and made two throwing errors, or booted two balls, or something else had gone wrong. I would sit there and that's all I thought about. He'd help me deal with it, because obsessing about that game wasn't going to help me get ready for the next one.

Once it got closer to the season, and my teammates started pulling for me and everyone started coming together as a team, it began to feel better. That's what made college baseball special. At the beginning we were all kind of enemies. We were young and we were learning our boundaries. We all wanted to do well individually, but in the end we understood that when you're on a team, you are all as one. That's when that team atmosphere comes into play and you just have to take it and hold on to it.

BESIDES ALL THE baseball, I had schoolwork to do. A thousand things were coming at me. I wasn't very good at school, but I took it seriously. I always showed up at class and worked hard. I just did shitty on the tests. I mean, that's how it was. I had to really work at just being able to handle it all.

As far as the fall of 2001 went, I'll never forget this: We had a team meeting and as I was walking out, Murph stopped me and said, "Hey, you're not playing any more fall games."

I was thinking, He's going to redshirt me. I came here to play right away. I'm not about to redshirt. I'll transfer somewhere else.

That was my first thought.

He said, "You're not playing in the fall because I want you to get in the weight room and get stronger."

I said, "Whatever, man."

I'd lifted weights before, in high school, but not the way I should have. Our entire team would go into the weight room and just do chests because we were all small guys and we wanted to look massive, which really never happened.

I started working out properly and probably put on ten pounds. We would go out and hit and I started to get stronger. We started using minus-three bats, which means the bats' weight in ounces is three fewer than their length in inches. They were a little heavier than the bats we used in high school, which were usually minus-five. I could feel that I was stronger. Sure enough, Murph stopped me and said, "Hey, you're going to be on our team. You're not going to redshirt."

Sweet!

THE LATE WINTER of 2002 rolled around and we started practicing. There were two second basemen and five shortstops now, after Coach Murphy had made some cuts. I didn't know where I was at. Nobody was telling me anything. I was just keeping my head down and playing as hard as I could. I didn't know what to expect.

Sure enough, the day before the January 31 season opener against Oregon State, my parents were coming up for the game and I didn't even know if I was on the team.

Murph pulled me aside and said, "Hey, you're batting second tomorrow and playing second base."

I said, "About a week ago you're telling me I'm the worst player on the planet. Our team must suck if you think I should be playing."

Murph just laughed at me.

The first game came and I went 2 for 4, with a walk and a run batted in. I scored three runs. I made two diving plays at second base. We ended up winning the game 13-5 and everything was great. But it still felt like things were coming at me at a thousand miles per hour.

As the season went on, Ian Kinsler, who's now with the Texas Rangers, ran into some trouble as our shortstop. He made some errors and Murph got down on him. And when Murph gets down on you, it's lights out. It's no joke.

Ian ended up getting benched by Murph, who moved me to third base because he didn't think I could play short. I was over at third base for ten games. I continued to hit well and hadn't made an error. I was playing great, we were still winning, but our shortstop, the guy who had replaced Ian, started making errors. So Ian went back in, and he was having a tough time. In the first game of three against Oklahoma in mid-March, Ian had two errors.

You could say I was kind of the last resort.

Here it was. The chance I'd waited for. I had played eight games at second base and sixteen at third base. From there on out, I played shortstop just about the rest of the season. My average freshman year was .347. We ended up losing in the regionals, and I ended up first-team all-PAC-Ten and first team freshman all-American, in a season that started with me not even sure I'd made the team. Ian transferred out to Missouri, where he played really well and was drafted by the Texas Rangers in 2003.

I learned a lot that year. One time I struck out on a slider, and when I came back to the dugout, Murph asked me how the pitch looked. I said, "Dude, it was *nasty*." A little later he pulled me aside and said, "If you're saying their pitcher is throwing nasty stuff, everybody else will think they can't hit it." From then on, when anybody asked me about the other pitcher, I'd say, "He sucks!" Then I started yelling at the pitchers from the dugout: "Man, you're *terrible*." They'd just look back at me from the mound.

Murph also taught me a lot about hitting. I'd step in the bucket when I was swinging—he called it "bailing and wailing"—and so he helped me make some small adjustments.

Murph also believed in what he called "corner hitting," which is to go down the right- or left-field lines instead of over the middle.

He liked to coach guys to hit the ball in front of outfielders instead of trying to power it over them.

Murph liked me, and one time when I was a freshman he told me that I reminded him of his good friend Mike Gallego, who had played in three World Series as a second baseman for the Oakland Athletics when I was a kid.

I said, "Mike Gallego? Are you shitting me?" Gallego had a career batting average under .240. I said, "Murph, is that the best you can do?" He just looked at me like he wanted to kick my ass again.

AFTER THE 2002 season, we had our final team meetings, and Murph said, "Hey, I want you to go play on Team USA—they invited you."

I didn't even know how that worked. There were invites all over the country and a lot of infielders were among those invited. Some of those guys are in big leagues now. Aaron Hill from Louisiana State, Conor Jackson from Cal, and Carlos Quentin from Stanford were all invited.

My freshman year, I had hit well, but not with a lot of power. I only had one home run, although I drove in sixty runs. So Murph said, "You need to do one thing for me: you need to lift weights. You're going to go play forty more games and you're going to look like you're sick."

I was like, "All right. That sounds good."

I tried out for the team and got blown up using a wood bat. I got a bone bruise because I'm so small. They didn't have a thirty-two-inch bat, like when I played in the Area Code Games, so it was a little different. But I hit some lasers and they all seemed impressed enough.

I ended up playing that summer with Team USA.

Team USA was a great experience, and I met some great teammates. We were going to play in Australia and Europe, and my teammates were some of the best college players out there.

It was when I was on Team USA that I also decided to give up my baseball scholarship.

I really wanted to get to the College World Series. There was a pitcher on Team USA named Ben Thurmond who had played at Winthrop and had sat out most of his junior year with an injury after being named a preseason All-American. Ben wanted to transfer to ASU for his senior year.

He could have been a big part of helping us win the national championship, but Coach Murphy had no more scholarships to give, and Ben couldn't afford to play at ASU without a scholarship. I called Murph and told him to give Ben mine.

I hadn't even told my parents. I called my mother and said, "I gave back my scholarship so we can get to the College World Series. I knew you wouldn't mind . . ."

My mother didn't seem surprised that I'd do something like that. She talked to my father and he said that was fine. He said he'd just sell some extra tires.

ON JULY 25, 2002, I was with Team USA playing in the "Honkbal Classic" in Haarlem, Netherlands, near Amsterdam. *Honkbal* is the Dutch word for baseball; this was an international tournament with teams from the Netherlands, South Africa, Cuba,

Japan, and Taipei. Before that, we'd been playing across the States. We were supposed to head to Italy in August for the twenty-seven-and-under World Baseball Championships.

I'd never traveled like that before, and it was an experience. I was just out of my freshman year of college and getting a new level of competition. The team was seven freshmen and twenty sophomores from around the country. A lot of those guys ended up in the major leagues: of the twenty-seven guys on the team, fifteen have made it to the majors. Our coach was Lelo Prado, who was the head coach at Louisville at the time.

In our game against Cuba, we were ahead with two outs in the ninth inning and some guy hit a rocket ground ball to me at short. I was ready for it, but then it bounced up and smashed into my eye. It broke six bones under and one above my eye—my whole eye socket was basically crushed.

From the second it hit me, everyone thought it was career ending. Rickie Weeks was playing left field in that game and he ran over. He was speechless. Looking at him looking at me, I knew I was in pretty bad shape.

I'd also gotten a concussion, so everything about that is hazy. I guess I walked off the field and then they took me to the hospital. But what I remember was waking up in the hospital. The doctors there had read the CT scan, and they were sending it to some doctors back in the United States to get it read as well. The diagnosis was a "right infraorbital rim fracture." The trainer from Team USA and the guy who ran the program stayed there in the hospital with me the whole night. The nurses had to wake me up every hour to make sure I was sleeping properly, given the concussion.

After a few days the swelling had gone down enough that I

could be released from the hospital. They put me on a flight home. Baseball was definitely over for that summer. For all I knew, it was over for good. I was eighteen years old.

The first leg of the flight was seven hours from Amsterdam to Boston. At Logan Airport in Boston, I had to get off the plane and switch flights. We'd packed to be away all summer, a two-and-a-half-month trip. I had all my bags, and all my baseball stuff. I had to go to another terminal and check in for my flight. It was the first time I'd ever been in Boston. I was hearing people talking in that Boston accent for the first time. It felt like I was still in a foreign country. I had sunglasses on to cover the eye. My whole face was bruised and swollen and my eye was slammed shut.

The woman at the airline counter looked at me and said, "Wow, what's wrong with your face?"

"None of your business, lady." She gave me this look.

I wouldn't be back in Boston for a few more years.

Next was six hours to Phoenix, then another flight up to California. I'd been traveling more than twenty-four hours, and I was in a lot of pain. When I got back to my parents, it felt like I was finally safe.

I couldn't open my eye for almost two weeks. It was one of those things where the doctors didn't know, because until the swelling came down in my eye, they didn't know if I would be able to see clearly, or even at all. I went to every eye specialist in the Phoenix area. They said I just had to wait.

I was back in my apartment at Arizona State, and for the next few days I was constantly checking my eye in the mirror. It was gross, oozing pus. It was like when you wake up in the morning and you have stuff in your eye, but this was at a much more rapid rate. Every fifteen or twenty minutes I was going to the mirror with a napkin to clean stuff out and try to see something. I couldn't run or work out or do anything physical to get my mind off things, because the doctors told me not to get any sweat in the eye. I just sat there on the couch, waiting.

I was nervous. I'd had a really good freshman year at Arizona State. I'd batted .347 and had begun to think that maybe I could succeed in this game. But besides that, baseball was all I'd ever wanted to do. It had never occurred to me what I would do if I weren't a ballplayer. It seemed that my career had been just about to get going, but now I was sitting on a couch wondering if I'd ever play again. I kept telling myself, Just wait. I had to force myself to be patient.

Sitting there watching TV, I kept working on my eye until I could get it to open just a little bit. The swelling had gone down to where I could just barely open the eyelid, but now it opened enough that something was coming through. I couldn't see much, but what I could see was clear and focused. I could see! It might have been one of the best feelings I've ever had. I was going to be able to continue doing what I loved, and it felt like I'd been given a new life.

The doctors had actually told me I was lucky, because my eyes are a little more sunken than average. They said that for some people whose eyes are set a little more outwardly, it would have destroyed their eyesight forever.

Once the swelling went down, I had surgery. The seams of the baseball had cut me badly. I had a gash under the eye, and even now I can touch under my eye and feel the bone sticking up. The surgeons went in and restructured things. It left a scar you can barely see. But at least they made me look even better than I already looked. I mean, I'm from California, so I needed my plastic surgery.

When the eye healed completely, I was fine.

It was like I was being given this second chance. I kept thinking how because of one bad hop of the baseball, it could have been over, right at the start.

But it would turn out there was damage done in a different way that year. Besides being left with a scar, I would find that the incident also left me with a fear I'd never had before.

MY SOPHOMORE YEAR started, and Coach Murphy sat me down and said, "Don't play any fall ball." The doctors wanted me not to sweat or move in a way that would make the blood flow too much to my eye. So for six weeks I sat back and watched the team play.

Coach Murphy decided that since I wasn't able to play, then after the six weeks of rest I should work out the whole off-season at the Athletes' Performance Institute in Tempe. I did that for those months, and you could tell I was growing up into my own body.

But the thing was, I didn't want to play infield. I had almost died. That ball could have gone right through my face. Basically, I had a complex about not wanting to put my nose in the ball. I was afraid to field a ground ball in case something like that happened again. I thought, I don't want that shit; put me in the outfield. In my head, I kept thinking about how I was only one ground ball away from never playing again.

The time came that the team was going to be taking ground

balls to get ready for the next season, and in my gut my feeling was, I don't really want to do this. It was so strange. I'd always had fun taking ground balls, but now I was scared. I didn't want to get hit anymore. It was like going back to when you're a little kid just learning to play, and you're terrified of the ball.

Coach Murphy said he wanted me to work with a sports psychologist he knew. He said, "I trust him, he's awesome, he'll get you out of it."

I said, "Okay, who is he?"

"Harvey Dorfman."

I said, "Who in the hell is Harvey Dorfman?" I had just turned nineteen and I had no idea what a sports psychologist was. I didn't know that Harvey Dorfman was the best sports psychologist there was, the best in the world. And he was close with Coach Murphy. In fact, Coach Murphy has a tattoo on his back of people who have inspired him to be the best he can be. That includes Bruce Springsteen, Muhammad Ali, Pat Tillman, and . . . Harvey Dorfman.

Murph was always big on mental toughness and thought Harvey could help me. He felt Harvey could tell me something that would help get my head straight.

Harvey came in that year to give a talk to the whole team about motivation. After his talk, they set it up so I could have a one-on-one with him. Coach Murphy had explained to him what my situation was, so Harvey and I sat down in the coach's office.

Harvey said to me, "So what's your problem? What is it that's bothering you?"

I said, "Well, I got knocked out by a ground ball—a concussion, six broken bones, plastic surgery, the whole gig."

Then I told him, "I don't want to take a ground ball. I'm afraid."

Harvey said, "Well, what are you afraid of?"

I said, "What the f— do you think I'm afraid of? If I get hit again in the face by a ground ball, it'll probably hurt a lot more than the last time."

He looked at me and said, "Yeah, it probably will."

He thought about it for a second and then said, "But weren't you *born* to play this game?"

I said, "Yeah, I am, I'd like to think so."

"Okay," he said. "So stop being a pussy and just go out and do it, then." It was like he was pulling this drill-sergeant shit.

He said, "If you're afraid of the ball, then why don't you go out and play short with a catcher's mask on? You're going to look like an idiot, and people will call you a pussy, but at least it'll all be over with, being afraid of the ball."

And I'm just staring at him and not saying anything. I'm just sitting there thinking, Harvey Dorfman's the man . . .

Harvey asked me what the worst thing that could happen was. "It already happened," he said. "And you got through it. What you're feeling is understandable. You're human. Anyone in your shoes would be this way."

I'd felt all along that it was unnatural for me to react the way I had. I'd never shied away from doing anything in my life. It felt like to be afraid was to be taking my manhood away.

From then on, it was done. That's because Harvey Dorfman had figured out who I was, and had figured out exactly what needed to be said. He matched his message with the person who needed to hear it, which is exactly why he's the best sports psychologist in the world. He's the kind of guy who can figure out your personality in five seconds. Talk about being born to do a job: Harvey was born to do what he does. Once he established that I was a little different and crazy, he attacked me in a way that was meant to bring out the best in me.

Now I go out there and put my mouth in front of the ball—it doesn't matter. I try to be fearless, and I try to have the attitude that what will happen, will happen. Harvey had a way of getting through to me that injury is a part of the job, and that overcoming the fears that hold you back is part of the job, too.

AS I SAID, the infield at Arizona State is hard packed. That sophomore season came, and I faced ground balls, and they came at me fast. I was lucky—one hit me in the jaw, and another in the neck. They hurt, but they were also no big deal. I knew after those that I was over the fear. Taking more and more ground balls in practice helped. The more reps I took, the better I felt. The better I felt, the more balls I wanted to take, almost obsessively. It was a marker of how I'd gotten past this fear that had been so huge.

The funny thing was, I think the injury had its effect on my game to a greater degree than I could have imagined: I ended up being so much more focused on ground balls, it improved my game way beyond what probably would have happened if I'd never been hurt that badly. In both my sophomore and junior years I would end up winning the National Collegiate Baseball Defensive Player of the Year award.

And that sophomore season was a turning point where I knew I could advance my career past college. I hit .404, I set a record in the Pac-10 for doubles, led the nation in five categories, and we were number two in the country.

Super-Regionals time came and they sent us to play a best-of-three series with the number-one team in the country, Cal State–Fullerton. So we drove to Fullerton, which had not lost a home game the whole season.

We lost the first game, won the second game, and lost the third game. I went 0 for 13 in the Super-Regional. I'd only gone hitless four games all season before this. They keyed on me and shut me down. They had the best pitching staff in the country, featuring future major leaguers Chad Cordero and Wes Littleton.

I felt personally responsible for what happened. My job all year had been to get on base and score runs. We had good hitters like Andre Ethier, Jeff Larish, and Travis Buck—we had five future big leaguers ourselves, all position players. So in my mind, I was the reason we didn't win. And after that season, I went through a stage where I said, "That's not going to happen anymore. If they can overpower me, I have to figure out how to out-think them. I have to find a better way."

I wanted very badly to get to the College World Series. I decided I'd work as hard as I knew how to get there. I wanted so badly for ASU to win.

Playing baseball there was a big responsibility. Coach Murphy demanded a lot out of you, and there were a lot of things going on. Yeah, it's a party school and all, but playing baseball for the Sun Devils, you don't have much time to do anything other than play ball and do schoolwork. Even though that didn't come easy, I tried to apply a work ethic to school the same way I did with baseball. I did all my homework. I showed up for class every day. But still, school was tough for me.

When I wasn't at the field, or going to practice, or trying to get better at baseball, I was probably at a tutor's or asking my team-mates how the hell to do a math problem or something like that, just trying to stay eligible. That was my biggest thing, to stay eligible.

Going to Arizona State was, in a lot of ways, the most fun time of my life, because I was always meeting different kinds of people. As an eighteen-year-old, or a nineteen- or twenty-year-old, you're on your own for the first time and you're just kind of growing up. You have to find a way to manage, asking yourself, "What am I going to eat for the night?"

Earlier in your life it's "I wonder what Mom is making for dinner tonight."

Now you're on your own and you need to find a way to make it all work. It wasn't all that hard for me, but it was still something to take on. At least I knew how to cook a few things, and I knew how to do my laundry. College wasn't a total culture shock.

However, there were some guys on the ASU team who couldn't do *anything* when they first got to school. I had a roommate my junior year who didn't know how to do any of that kind of stuff. Instead of learning to do laundry, he'd just go out and buy a whole bunch of new underwear, something like once a month. But that's what it is in school—you rely on people to help you learn. I ended up helping him do his laundry. That was kind of a joke, that I was teaching someone else how to do his laundry, but that's what made it fun.

My life was changing in a lot of ways. I had moved away from Woodland when I went off to Arizona State, and I had never really gone back. Playing baseball at Arizona State was a year-round thing, but I knew it was also time for me to move on from my hometown. I remember my father saying to me, when I left for Arizona, that it was time to go off and find my success. I didn't plan to be coming back, because in a sense, the only way that could happen is if I hadn't fulfilled the dreams I was setting out to accomplish.

Later, when I was playing minor-league ball, I still chose to spend the off-season in Arizona. By then it felt like home to me, and Coach Murphy had become like a second father to me. Arizona would be where I became an adult, and it would become the place I'd call a home, for all the right reasons.

I grew apart from people I'd known in Woodland. I also grew apart from my older brother. He went his way and associated with his people, and I went my way and associated with the new people in my life. His baseball career was over—he'd had a bad ankle injury playing at Shasta Junior College. After a time, we didn't have a lot in common, and I didn't see much of him.

That was sad, because when I was a little kid, I'd always looked up to him so much. But I also had come to a point where I was just trying to live my life in the way I wanted. I'd always been a good kid and had never given my parents much of a problem, and that was probably because I liked to live my life very simply. I loved baseball. It's what I poured all my energy into during my whole time at ASU, and later, too, wherever baseball took me. I didn't let my life get very complicated.

MY JUNIOR YEAR at Arizona State, right before the 2004 draft, we had Scout Day. That's when major-league scouts come in on a specific day and the players can show their stuff.

On Scout Day, all the draft-eligible players do a series of drills, catch and throw, run a sixty-yard dash, and take batting practice. Jeff Larish was there, because as a junior at Arizona State he was up for the draft, and was rated high, the number-eleven player overall. Jeff had also been my teammate on Team USA. He had originally come in as another shortstop competing with me, and they had moved him to corner infield: third base and first base. I'd lucked out there, because he was a number-one position prospect.

Everyone was there to see Jeff, but there were about a dozen guys out there to show what they had. While the scouts were there, I guess they figured, "Why not look at the little shortstop, too?"

And, you know, it only takes one or two guys to like you.

That year, Jeff was struggling. He'd gotten a wrist injury that had really affected him. He'd hit .372 his sophomore year, but in 2004 it dropped down to .308. It all got to him, you could tell. They put so much pressure on him that year, pressure to be *everything*. He was twenty-one years old. You can't do that to a kid at that age.

And I guess because Jeff had to bear all the pressure of the expectations, it took any pressure off me that would have been there.

I did okay at Scout Day. In late April, we were playing at Wichita State. I knew that the Red Sox had their first pick in the second round of the draft, the sixty-fifth pick overall. I had heard Jeff talk about it, because he was slipping and hoped the Sox might get him with their pick. He said, "Supposedly, [general manager] Theo Epstein's here today, with their scouting director." The Red Sox were playing at Kansas City a few days later, so they had come to the game. I said, "Really? Boston? That's awesome."

Me, I didn't know anything about the East Coast, and didn't

want to know anything about the East Coast. For me, it was always the Giants—that was my thing and I didn't care about anything else. But I was happy the Red Sox had come to look at Jeff.

That day, though, I put on an absolute line-drive clinic. And I made four diving plays. It was probably one of the best games of my life. I went 4 for 4, with two home runs and two doubles, put a pickoff play on to save the game—just did everything right. It was like it was meant to be.

But at the end of the year, even though I was an All-American and a Golden Spikes finalist, and I had met with a lot of teams, Boston wasn't one of them. I never talked to them. I thought, Damn! If that guy Theo was really there, you'd think he would like me a little bit. I mean, draft me in whatever round, but . . .

I had heard people say I might be drafted in the first round, because my numbers were good. This was the year the book *Moneyball* came out, creating a whole new statistical look at prospects. Things like on-base percentage and slugging percentage were given more emphasis. I'd hit .393 my junior year. My OBP was .502. One of the statistics that seemed to interest people was that I didn't strike out much, and in my junior year I'd walked something like thirty times more than I'd struck out. Statistically, I was feeling like what I had measured up. But, as always, my size seemed to hold people back. Still, I was thinking, Somebody just draft me. I don't care.

My size always seemed to come into it. There was this idea that I didn't look like a big-league ballplayer. Some people would ask me if I wished I were big. I never did. I always wanted to be a miniature badass.

Draft day—June 8, 2004—came. I remember sitting there with

Jeff and some of the other draft-eligible guys in the coach's office. My parents had flown in and they said, "You never know; if you get drafted we'll help move you out." Coach Murphy was saying, "You really don't need to play another year of college baseball. You've played three years and you've dominated." So I'm thinking, Okay, whatever, and then one of the coaches is in the other room yelling "Yeah, yeah!" and I'm assuming they drafted Jeff, and I'm thinking, Sweet. Then I hear them saying my name. It didn't register. I stood there thinking, Shit . . . that's *me* . . .

My agent at the time was Bobby Witt, who had pitched for sixteen years in the big leagues. He called me and said, "Hey, the Red Sox drafted you—you're their first pick."

I thought, I guess maybe they did like me.

JEFF ENDED UP getting picked in the thirteenth round by the Dodgers. He decided to stay another year at ASU and prove that 2004 was just a fluke. He ended up starring in the College World Series in 2005 and getting drafted in the fifth round by the Tigers, and came up to the majors with Detroit in 2008.

But I wouldn't be there for it. I was heading to something completely different than I had come to know at Arizona State.

My agent said that the next step was to get a signing bonus, because I was their top pick. And I was saying, "I'll sign the contract today if they send me right to Double A." I was crazy. I didn't care what money I made as long as I could get to the big leagues.

Bobby said, "Relax. You just got drafted today."

I told him I didn't give a shit. I was going nuts. I wanted to be playing pro ball.

• • •

THE PROCESS OF signing that first contract turned out to be kind of confusing. Right away, one of the Red Sox scouts said to me that they had "overdrafted" me, and why didn't I just sign for what they were offering me? It seemed low, though.

I told him, "Dude, I'm not here to break the bank, I'm here to play baseball. I don't give a shit. Just sign me for slot money." Slot money is the amount of signing-bonus money Major League Baseball recommends for someone drafted at a certain pick, or "slot." I told this scout I was ready to sign for that. My mentality has always been that I'm going to succeed at anything I'm going to do—that's just the way I have to think. So I said, "Just sign me, and let me play, and the next time I hear from you, you're going to be asking me to get you tickets for a Red Sox game."

The Red Sox came up with a little bit, but it wasn't close to being slot money. And I said, "Okay, when you get to slot money, let me know, and I'll go out and play and kick everybody's ass. Until then, just leave me alone, because I'm working out right now getting myself *jacked*."

I went to Reno, Nevada, to start hitting. I had some buddies who were playing pro ball and I could hit at the facility up there. I was just waiting to sign. The Red Sox wouldn't move up their offer to slot money and it was starting to make me mad.

I would watch some of the Red Sox games on TV and vent my frustration. I was ready to go compete and I was left sitting there, and it pissed me off. On TV, Nomar Garciaparra would be playing short and he would make an error or he wouldn't get a guy on the throw to first. Of course, errors and things happen. I don't think

Nomar even made that many errors that season, but every time I turned the Red Sox game on, it seemed like he was making one. Being in this mood, I would get all pissed off, and so when the Red Sox area scout would call me up and say something negative toward me I would say, "Listen, your guy is out there making errors in Boston, so why don't you sign me because I can make that play that Nomar just didn't."

I'd be yelling at him, because that's just how I was about getting the contract done so I could get on the field.

Another week went by with no news. Finally, they called— "Here's slot money, $575,000." I was fine on that. But now my agent starts in, saying, "Don't sign yet, you can get a million." He said there was a guy who'd been picked a few years before me at nearly the same slot who had gotten a million dollars from the Red Sox. It was a pitcher, Jon Lester, who was drafted fifty-seventh overall in 2002. And he was only some eighteen-year-old high school kid!

I understood that my agent's job was to get me the most money, but I said, "You know what? I'm ready to just go play. I don't want to mess this thing up." My first thought was, I don't care about making money in the draft. I want to make it actually playing in the big leagues. That had stuck in my mind since I'd visited some agencies and one of them had told me that. *The money comes from showing people you can play the game, not from being drafted.* I'd thought, I like that. I'll write that down. It made sense.

So I signed.

6

Salad Days in the Sally League

A few weeks after I was drafted, and once I signed, the Red Sox called and wanted to set up a conference call with the media. And as I said, I didn't know the first thing about the East Coast. I'd been in Boston that one time, dragging my stuff through Logan Airport with one eye swollen shut, thinking that people there talked funny.

I got on the phone and waited. First, the media was interviewing Theo. I was just sitting on my phone in Arizona, listening. The situation in Boston was that Nomar Garciaparra, the Red Sox shortstop, was hurt and not playing. The Red Sox were playing three against the Yankees and Nomar had made three errors in the first two games, and the Red Sox had lost both. And the night before, the Red Sox had played the third game at Yankee Stadium and this was the extra-inning game where the Yankee shortstop, Derek Jeter, had gone diving into the stands after a foul ball and gotten his face messed up. The Yankees won the game, which Nomar sat out.

Even though the conference call was supposed to be about me signing, they were only asking Theo questions about the Nomar situation. But then I realized that they were asking him the *same* questions, over and over and over. *Is Nomar going to play tonight? Is Nomar going to play? When is Nomar going to play?*

Theo answered the question. He said that Nomar had a mandatory day off.

The next six questions were the same question that Theo had just answered.

I was on this conference call, sitting there on my phone listening, and now I was thinking, These people are crazy. These people are nuttier than me.

Finally they finished that topic, and now they were ready to ask me questions about my signing, and what I was going to do for the Red Sox. And sure enough, they started asking me the same questions over and over: *How do you feel about the pressure of playing in Boston? Do you think you can handle the pressure of Boston? There's a lot of pressure playing for the Red Sox—can you handle it?*

I'm thinking, Is there a problem with this phone line? Are you not hearing me? Do you want me to give the same answer but worded differently? It was my first taste of exactly how intense Boston is about the Red Sox. I didn't know yet that in Boston the team is basically God, with Ted Williams a close second.

And I kept saying, "Dude, I'm just here to win baseball games, I don't care—next question, next question." I'd never even done a real interview before. I didn't even know what I was saying. The best I could offer was "Look, you throw a fastball at me, I can hit it very hard. What else is there to say? Is there anything else to say?"

• • •

I HAD A signed contract and I was ready to go play baseball, wherever that was going to be. They told me they were sending me to Augusta, Georgia. My first thought was, I don't even know where Augusta, Georgia, is.

The Augusta GreenJackets play in the South Atlantic League—the "Sally League"—which is low Class-A ball. The Masters golf tournament is of course the biggest thing in Augusta, and the winner receives a green jacket, so that's why it's the baseball team's name.

I will never forget that trip to Augusta: I got on a plane in Sacramento, ready to go, and ended up sitting in the plane on the runway for five and a half hours. There was a problem, but they wouldn't let us off the plane. We didn't take off until ten o'clock at night, and I was supposed to fly into Atlanta and get a connecting flight into Augusta. But I'd already missed my connecting flight from Atlanta before we had even taken off in Sacramento.

I got to Atlanta and slept on the floor in the airport. I had three bags. Early in the morning, I got a flight to Augusta. When I got there, I called Beau Vaughan, who was pitching with the Green-Jackets and had been a teammate of mine at Arizona State the year before. I asked him where a good place to stay was. I didn't really even know what to do.

He said, "Yeah, no problem, I got a place right here for you." I'm thinking, Sweet! He said he had a bed waiting for me.

But the thing is, Beau's a little different. I love the guy to death, but he's just not like everybody else.

After twenty-four hours of travel time, I got to his place, and I was tired. Beau brought me in and showed me my bed. But it wasn't exactly a bed: It was one of those mattresses you float in a swimming pool. I mean, my bed had cup holders.

Beau said, "Yeah, man, you can sleep right here. Just lay this thing on the floor."

And I said to Beau, "Dude, how am I supposed to be laying out rockets when I'm sleeping on this shit every night?"

He looked at me and he said, "Dude, just hold on a minute . . . I mean, this is the best we've *got* in Augusta . . ."

Augusta was literally a thousand miles away from Fenway Park. Some guys had been the stars on every team they'd ever played for, but this was as far as they were going to get. You had to get yourself ready for the long haul. I figured I was going to have to deal with adversity. I ended up sleeping on this *thing*. My blanket was a towel, which Beau was actually still using at the time. No pillow, either.

The fact was that most of the guys on that team would never play higher than A ball, and others would finish their careers at Double A, and a few more might get to Triple A and never make it to the major leagues. The oldest guys on the team were twenty-four and twenty-five, and they were already figuring out that it just wasn't going to happen. Some guys hadn't been drafted and had signed as free agents hoping for something to happen, or maybe just wanting to continue playing baseball as long as anyone would let them, just for the love of the game.

I came in ready to prove myself all over again.

I practiced with the team for the next five days, but they wouldn't let me play. I didn't know what was going on. I'd practice, and then sit for the games. This was discouraging. I was here ready to play. I went up to the manager after the fifth day and I said that

I guess you could say that I loved the game,
and the Sox, from an early age

Soccer was another one of my favorite
sports

Batting in the living room was pretty
common

5

6

ABOVE: Woodland High was where I decided that baseball was what I wanted to do for the rest of my life

LEFT: Safe on base

7

At Arizona State I played shortstop, batted .384 lifetime, and was
named both all-American and Defensive Player of the Year

ASU head coach Pat Murphy taught me a lot about hitting and lifting weights

Practicing at spring training with Red Sox DH David Ortiz and manager Terry "Tito" Francona

Hanging out with my role-models-turned-teammates Mike Lowell and Alex Cora

13

The happiest day of my life that didn't involve a bat in my hands: Kelli and I were married in November 2006

14

Enjoying a snow day with my friends and family

15

I played at the Triple-A level for the Pawtucket Red Sox for the last half of the 2005 season and the first half of the 2006 season

16

On the field at Fenway Park

17

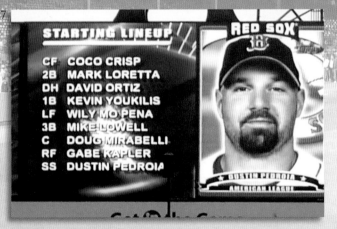

The first time I got up to bat in the major league, they showed the wrong picture on the scoreboard; that's a picture of Dustan Mohr, who played for the Red Sox in 2006

Accepting the 2007 AL
Rookie of the Year award

With Kelli, just after receiving the 2008
American League MVP award

Admiring the 2007 Commissioner's
Trophy

Celebrating our 2007 American League Championship Series win
with the guys I came up through the minor leagues with. Left to right:
Clay Buchholz, Jonathan Papelbon, Brandon Moss, Jon Lester,
Manny Delcarmen, Jacoby Ellsbury, Bryan Corey

At the 2007 World Series victory parade with my teammates and
our families. Left to right: Eric Hinske with his wife, Kathryn, and
daughter Ava; Kelli and me; Kevin Youklis and his now-wife, Enza

if he didn't put me in the lineup I was going to leave. I was going to head home.

The manager was Chad Epperson. He'd been a catcher in the minor-league systems of the Mets, Braves, and Red Sox before turning to managing. He was a laid-back guy, so when I told him I might leave, he just listened to me.

He told me I had to wait. He said the organization had told him not to put me in until I got myself in shape.

I said, "What do you mean 'get in shape'? I *am* in shape . . ."

He looked at me and laughed. "Your body's terrible. What the hell are you talking about?"

I remember in those first few days overhearing Eppy talking to the Red Sox farm director, Ben Cherington. Ben said, "How's our top draft pick doing?"

Eppy said, "Well, he's not the biggest guy in the world . . . his batting practice hasn't been very good . . . I guess he's okay at shortstop . . . So this guy was really your first pick?"

But they finally decided to put me in at shortstop. First game comes, and I go 4 for 4 with two walks. It was a thirteen-inning game, and I was on base six times. We ended up winning the game. I scored five runs, I think I drove in three, and made all my plays at shortstop. Afterward, Eppy said to the bosses, "Hey, looks like we have a real ballplayer on our hands . . . Just don't ever watch him take batting practice."

Twelve games went by and we were on a winning streak. We went from last place to playing the first-place team in a three-game set with first place at stake. We won two out of three, so we were still one game out. But we were kicking some butt. Beau had told me, when I first got to Augusta, that there wasn't much of a team atmosphere like we'd had back at Arizona State. But once I'd gotten there, it did feel like a team. Everybody had been telling me minor-league ball sucks, but here I was having a pretty good time.

Not that playing minor-league ball at that level wasn't tough. In those kinds of leagues, the biggest nights that fans came out for were Fifty-Cent Hot Dog Night and 4-H Night and Two-Dollar Beer Night. The players were all nineteen- and twenty- and twenty-one-year-old kids nobody had ever heard of, and most of them weren't ever going to get to the big leagues.

After that road trip, I went and got some groceries, came back home, and got myself all set up in my little lounge area. I was just settling in when I got a phone call—the organization. I was going to Sarasota. I said, "Sarasota, where?" They said it was in Florida. Well, sweet!

I was going there because Hanley Ramirez, the top shortstop prospect in the Red Sox organization, was getting moved to Double A. I was in and out of the Sally League in twelve games. I'd had exactly fifty at-bats, and I'd hit exactly .400.

ON I WENT to the Sarasota Red Sox in the Florida State League. It was still Class-A ball, but a step up, what's called "High A." And we got on a winning streak there. We went from third place to first place. I was playing there for Todd Claus, and he was more like a college manager, with a lot of high intensity compared to how laid-back Eppy had been in Augusta.

At Sarasota, I met and played with the guys I'd go on to play with on the Red Sox. We had Jonathan Papelbon and Jon Lester and Manny Delcarmen pitching, and we had Brandon Moss and

David Murphy. We weren't really an A team, we were more like Double A or even Triple A. We began to get to know each other. There were a lot of personalities on that team. Pap had his personality, which was intense, while Jon Lester was a much quieter guy. Manny Delcarmen drove around in this rice-rocket car. David Murphy just liked to be quiet and watch his movies. Brandon Moss was twenty and the most immature guy in the world, but everybody loved him as soon as they met him. We started getting used to each other at a young age. I think that helped. We would all go to Double A together, then we'd start seeing guys get called up to Triple A, and by the time we all got up to Boston, we were already family.

But back then, Todd Claus was saying, "Don't worry about getting to Boston, worry about winning here in Sarasota, right now." It put everybody's mind-set on the immediacy of each game, and not the longer haul.

We knew we were far from the big stage at that point. In Sarasota some nights, we could be playing in front of fifteen people. The city was great and the weather was good, but you talk about the worst atmosphere ever to play in—there would be literally a couple of dozen people there sometimes. Ed Smith Stadium in Sarasota was the Cincinnati Reds' spring training field, and it seated 7,500 people. But it seemed that summer like there were never more than five hundred people in the stands, and usually a lot fewer.

In college, I had played in front of five thousand people per game. At Arizona State, we always had a packed house, with everybody going crazy. It wasn't very hard to get pumped up for a game. Now I'd be out there on the field in Sarasota on a hot late-summer night, thinking about how I'd had more family in the stands at my

Arizona State games than in the entire stadium that night. It wasn't all that much fun most of the time. On those nights, playing in the Florida State League, you had to pull the intensity up from inside yourself.

I WAS PLAYING well in Sarasota. I started out slow, hitting .260 or so, but then I did better. I played a total of thirty games there and finished the season hitting somewhere around .340. But our season got cut short because Hurricane Ivan was about to hit in the beginning of September. So they sent all of us home. But then, at my parents' in California, I got a call from Ben Cherington. He was inviting me to take batting practice with the big-league team. In Boston. At Fenway Park.

My family and I flew in from California for it. My mom and dad came. I took batting practice for two days, hitting in the first group, and I started hitting some bombs. Standing at home plate, I looked at the Green Monster and felt like I could touch it. I dug into the batter's box and started launching balls on the Coca-Cola bottle up above the wall.

One of the people there watching was Johnny Pesky, who'd played shortstop for the Red Sox back in the 1940s and '50s. Johnny was a fixture with the team, and at that time he still dressed for games, hit fungos for outfield practice, and sat in the dugout during games. He was eighty-four years old but still in full uniform, number 6. I was just raking, and he stood by the cage yelling, "There goes another one! There goes another one!"

Afterward he came up and introduced himself, and gave me a lot of encouragement. That was awesome.

I got to hang with the big-league players and take some ground balls. I got to talk a little to the media.

They seemed excited I was there. They seemed to like that I was a homegrown guy, coming up through the Red Sox farm system. And there were a lot of us like that. It was clear later on that it mattered. By 2007, when I was playing on the big stage, I was playing with a lot of guys I'd come up through the system with. We were all able to help each other adapt to the environment.

I was excited for my parents, too. They'd never been on a big-league field. I was glad they were there to see it.

That night we all went out to dinner in Boston. Ben came and said he had good news and he wanted my family to hear it: they were going to send me to go play in the Arizona Fall League.

Here I am, weighing about 140 pounds, and worn down from the year, but still not tired of baseball. Sweet!

Then he said, "But we're going to put you on a taxi squad."

"What the hell is a taxi squad?"

"It means you're going to play Wednesdays and Saturdays."

I was pissed. What the hell was I going to do with myself the other five days if I wasn't playing baseball?

He said I could just take batting practice and ground balls on my off days. I said, All right, whatever. I'll go there and kick ass on Wednesdays and Saturdays, then shut it down on the other days. On the off days I'll go out and hit and take ground balls and figure out a way to kill the next twenty-three hours waiting to go again.

I joined my team, the Scottsdale Scorpions, and it was competitive. But it was when I also saw that I could really get to the big leagues. I only had sixty at-bats, because I could only play Wednesdays and Saturdays, but I hit about .280. Russell Martin (now the starting catcher with the Dodgers) and I were the only taxi-squad guys, and our team went 17-1 on Wednesdays and Saturdays. We made sure to tell everybody about that. Rickie Weeks was on that squad, and Conor Jackson, and Carlos Quentin, and a lot of other good guys, but Russ and I would say, "Don't worry, guys, Wednesday and Saturday are coming up, and we can get you guys a W then—you stiffs just mess it up and we have to come in and fix it." It was a great year.

It was weird being back in Arizona just a few months after I'd left for Augusta. All my closest friends were still at Arizona State. I think there were only three guys who left the year I left, so everyone was still on the team at ASU. Also, when I found out I was going to the fall league, I actually came back to the same apartment building I'd lived in for the three years I played at ASU.

During my time at ASU, everyone had made fun of me because I never moved. I never moved anything. I am who I am and that's it. So, now I called up the landlord and asked to move back in. I had signed for a little bit of money, and while the building wasn't the nicest place, it was fine for me, and conveniently located across the street from the campus. The landlord, Boomer, was awesome, a hilarious guy. We would talk sports all the time. I felt comfortable there, and all my buddies came back to see me.

ONE DAY A friend said, "Hey, there's this girl I know, and she and her friends want to come and check out one of your fall-league games. I'm friends with four of them."

He also mentioned, "They're all hot, too."

I said, "Okay, sweet."

Now, I'm not that good-looking a guy, but I knew I had a pretty good personality, so I was thinking, Maybe I can pull something here.

I got them all tickets to the game, which was in Peoria, a suburb all the way on the other side of Phoenix from Tempe. They had to drive forty-five minutes, and they came with this friend of mine. I went 4 for 4 in the game and I was raking. They probably thought I was good. Maybe that helped me out a little bit.

These girls were all in a sorority at ASU. About a week later, they were having a formal event and one of the girls didn't have a date, so she asked me to go to it on Saturday. I was playing in the fall league—Wednesdays and Saturdays! But I had a day game that Saturday.

"Okay, I'll go with you," I said.

One of the other girls, Kelli Hatley, was going to the event with another guy, but they were just friends, not dating or anything. I headed over to the sorority after my game and hung out with all of them and had fun.

My date was really nice, but sparks weren't flying. Kelli was just sitting there so I started talking to her and we hit it off right away. After that night, we started hanging out more. Then I asked her out on a couple of dates and everything was going great.

That's how it started, but it was kind of weird. I had spent three years at ASU and never met Kelli. I had left ASU not knowing where I was headed in my life, where the game of baseball was going to take me. Then three months later I was back, and Kelli and I met.

She knew the minor-league baseball season was coming up and that I had to leave. So it was just one of those deals where you stay together and do the long-distance thing. But it all worked out well. Every day I would call her and we would talk. We were involved in each other's everyday lives; we knew what was going on. That year when I played in Portland and Pawtucket made us stronger as a couple, more able to get through stuff together.

Soon after I first met Kelli, we were swimming one day and I noticed a big scar on her leg. At first I was afraid to ask her about it. I thought, Did she get stabbed or something? I didn't know what the hell it was.

When I asked, Kelli said she had been addicted to the sun. She loved being in the sun and that was one of the reasons she moved to Arizona from Chicago. As a kid, she was always tanning. She started going to tanning booths when she was fourteen and would just bake herself. She worked in a water park all summer in high school, and never used sunscreen.

During her freshman year of college, she had been on a spring-break trip with her family to the Cayman Islands when she noticed a reddish mole on her right leg. A doctor cut it out and tested it. The doctor came back and said Kelli was the youngest patient she'd ever had with stage II melanoma. The tumor underneath the mole was the size of an egg. They had to remove a big chunk of lymph nodes from her leg to be sure the melanoma wouldn't spread. That procedure left her with a scar about three inches long.

However, she kept going out in the sun after the surgery, too. She was young enough to think that she could just keep on doing what she was doing. But two years after that first surgery she had an atypical mole removed from her neck, along the clavicle. I could barely see that because the doctors had done a great job, but to have it come back like that was scary. It's one of those things that you aren't aware of when it happens, that you sometimes can't see.

By the time I met Kelli, she'd mostly learned to take care of herself. But it wouldn't be the last time she'd have to deal with it.

THAT FALL OF 2004, the Red Sox won their first World Series since 1918.

I followed their amazing run, because I love baseball and was already part of the organization, but I kept a bit distant from it. Once I had signed and started playing in Augusta and Sarasota, I would try to follow the Red Sox, but it wasn't my main objective to watch the big team. I was more worried about myself and trying to climb up through the minor-league system.

When you're in the minors you put blinders on and try to get your ass to the big leagues as soon as possible. When the Sox won the World Series, did I care? Yeah, it was great. They hadn't won the World Series in like, hell, a billion years. It was great for the city and great for the fans. Red Sox Nation blew up into something much bigger.

But a lot of guys end up playing for a team other than the one that drafted them. People get moved around all the time. I was a teammate with a lot of guys in the minors who ended up playing for other teams in the majors. For example, Hanley Ramirez was traded to the Florida Marlins in a deal that brought the Red Sox another guy who's turned out to be a great teammate, Mike Lowell. So it was better to keep focused on what was right in front of me, because I had some control over that. Doing that and playing to the best of my abilities was the way to determine where I'd be in the future.

I'm not saying the 2004 playoffs weren't fun to watch, what with Pedro Martinez, Curt Schilling and the bloody sock, Damon and

Millar, all those guys. Besides, that 2004 team changed the mind-set for everybody who would follow them onto the field at Fenway. From then on, nobody who came to the Red Sox would have to play under the pressure of "You have to break the Curse." Those winning players of 2004 had it a lot tougher than the Sox teams that played in the wake of that success.

Ben Cherington

Senior Vice President and

Assistant General Manager

Boston Red Sox

One of the things we do in minor-league spring training every year is meet individually with each player to talk about development goals and give each player a realistic sense of where he stands and what he should expect at the end of spring training.

For some players, this means telling them they're competing for a job. For others, it might mean telling them they're going to start the year in High A or Double A, and that spring training should be about working on specific things and preparing for the season.

Dustin's first spring training with us was in 2005. I was the farm director at the time. He had signed in 2004 and played some in Augusta and Sarasota, which at the time were our Low-A and High-A teams, respectively. Usually, a newly signed player will go to instructional league after the season. But we felt Dustin was advanced enough to go to the Arizona Fall League that year to get some additional at-bats. Since instructional league is usually the place where I would start to really get to know the new players, I didn't know Dustin very well when he reported to spring training in '05.

With every player in the minor leagues, it's our job to identify their limitations and help them work on them so they have the best chance to get to the big leagues. We talk about those things in our individual meetings in spring training and then throughout the year. Dustin was so advanced in so many areas of the game that our meeting with him in spring training was going to be a little different than it was for most players. He already controlled the strike zone, he already had great defensive instincts, and he already knew how to run the bases. The biggest thing for us at that time was to help Dustin figure out how to stay strong through a full professional season. He needed to improve his body composition and develop a daily routine that would allow him to stay strong. When these are the biggest things to work on with a player, it means the player development process is pretty easy. Most players have a huge laundry list of limitations to work on. With Dustin, there were just a couple.

So I sat down with Dustin for our meeting. First we made some small talk. We talked about his off-season, talked a little about how the Arizona State Sun Devils were going to do that spring, and so forth. Again, I didn't really know him that well at this time. But I wanted to get to know him. We talked for a while about what he could do to stay strong through the full season. I told him we thought he needed to make some adjustments with his conditioning, and maybe even his diet—to Dustin's credit, he has done a remarkable job reshaping his body over the years and is now one of the best-conditioned players in our organization, which no doubt helps him be a great player in October.

By this time he was starting to look at me a little funny. It was like he was thinking to himself, Who the hell is this guy in the khakis and golf shirt telling me what to do?

We then started talking about where he might start the season. We hadn't decided whether he would go back to Sarasota or start the year in Portland [Maine]. We knew he was an advanced player but that he only had about forty professional games under his belt at the time. The typical path for a good college player from a major program is to go to High A in his first full season. The fact that we were even considering Portland was actually a credit to Dustin.

He didn't see it that way.

When I told him we hadn't decided where he would start the season, he looked at me like I had three heads. Not only was this guy he barely knew telling him he had to get in better shape, but now I was telling him he might go back to A ball to start the season. He didn't say anything at first, but the look on his face said, "What the f— are you talking about?" He was clearly agitated, so I gave him some of the old player-development clichés: "It doesn't matter where you start the year, it matters where you finish" and "Control what you can control." Dustin didn't seem to be buying it.

Finally he said, "I don't know why the hell you guys would want to send me back to A ball."

If most minor-league players said that in their first individual meeting with the farm director, it would have been false bravado. And it would not have been taken well. If anything, most times this would have guaranteed that the player *would* have started the year in A ball, because it would have been seen as a sign of immaturity.

I'm not sure why, but I had to work hard to stop from laughing when Dustin said it. It was so clear he actually believed it. He wasn't pissed so much as he was wondering how we could be so stupid as to consider sending him back to A ball. Like, *Haven't you seen me play?*

We finished the meeting and Dustin left my office. As a farm director, you spend a lot of your time worrying about things. How is this player doing? Is this player making progress on his goals? Is he having problems off the field? How long will it take him to get back from his injury? Do we have enough pitching in Portland tomorrow?

After that meeting, I knew there was one less player I had to worry about.

7

Climbing the Ladder

I started training again that winter, right after the fall league
ended. I lived in Reno by myself. There was a trainer up there
I'd met through one of my buddies at Arizona State. I wanted
to train at a high elevation, to help my lungs and help me get in
better shape. Reno is at an altitude of 4,500 feet. I had read that
Brian Urlacher, a linebacker for the Chicago Bears, had done that.
I thought, Dude, if Brian Urlacher does that, then I want to be as
crazy as him and do that, too. So I was up there in Reno busting
my butt. Another reason I wanted to be training up there is that it
gets real cold and snowy. And I had already decided that my goal
for the 2005 season was to be playing at Portland, Maine. The
Portland Sea Dogs are the Red Sox's Double-A team, and that's
where I planned to be. Given that I was a guy from California,
where the weather didn't get that cold, and that I'd played college
baseball in Arizona, I knew I needed to adjust. I wanted to be up
in Reno hitting outside in the freezing cold, so that when I got to
Portland to start the season, I'd be ready to rock. I would go out-

side every day and hit in the snow. I'd be out getting my work done in snowstorms. Everybody thought I was crazy.

Spring training 2005 came around and I went to the Sox camp in Fort Myers, Florida, figuring I was ready to go for a good season in Double A. I thought my 2004 performance, especially in the fall league, made it definite I'd get moved up.

But then I got into a run-in with Ben Cherington, our farm director. At the time, I guess I really didn't know how it all worked.

Ben called me and met with me, and during our talk he said, "Hey, we might want to send you back to High-A ball."

It wasn't what I'd been expecting to hear. I was really upset. After all the work I'd done getting ready, I didn't want to deal with anything negative. I thought, This is *bullshit*.

I said, "But Ben, wait, this is day one. And you can't judge me on day one." I'd been focused all winter, getting ready to play Double A in Portland. I kind of went nuts on him. He must have thought, This guy's insane. I mean, he's thinking, We've got a twenty-year-old kid in here literally going insane. How the hell am I going to stop him from going nuts?

On the third day of spring training, I was told to come over to the big-league camp, and I was thinking it was probably to fill in for one of the starters for a day. But in fact manager Terry "Tito" Francona wanted to have a talk with me. Tito called me into his office. I was scared to death of him at that time, because I didn't know him the way I know him now. Apparently he wasn't too happy.

Tito sat me down and said, "Hey, man, you can't be yelling at the farm director."

"I didn't."

He said, "Yeah, well, you kind of did."

I said, "Well, maybe I kind of did, but I just thought it was unfair that he didn't give me the opportunity to go to Double A, after one day of being in camp. And if he did make a decision based on one day, then just let me know what that one day is going to be, and I'll kick ass and show everybody I should be in Double A."

Tito was looking at me as if to say, "Who the hell is this guy? I've got other things to worry about than this little shit."

I ended up going back to the minor-league complex, and playing for a week, getting back into baseball shape and hitting the ball well. At the end of the week, Ben called me back into his office and said, "Okay, Dustin, we're going to send you to Double A." I sat there thinking, Good, it's about time you figured it out. I didn't say that to him, but I was pretty sure he could tell that that was exactly what I was thinking.

Then he said, "But the thing is, you're going to be playing second base. Hanley Ramirez will be playing shortstop in Portland. Do you have any experience playing second?"

"I played around ten games at second base in college."

"Is that going to be a problem?"

I said, "Hell no!"

He said, "You and Hanley are going to play up the middle, then. Does that work for you?"

"Hell yeah, it works for me. Put us in and we'll go kick everybody's asses."

IT WENT WELL right from the start with the Sea Dogs. Hanley and I started turning two together, and it came naturally to me, playing second base. The more reps I took, the better I got.

The regular season at Portland started, and the first time we played up there, I was struck by the wild atmosphere—at Portland, you could get a rough feeling of what it was going to be like if you ever did get to Boston. It's a big step, being among the Red Sox maniacs. Hadlock Field, where the Sea Dogs play, has about seven thousand seats, and most nights it was packed, and it was rocking. Hadlock has a left-field wall that replicates the Green Monster at Fenway Park. They call it "the Maine Monster." It is the same height, the same color. There is a Coca-Cola bottle up above, and they have even put a Citgo sign above the wall like the one that's in Kenmore Square just over the Green Monster. It's a hundred miles from the Maine Monster to the Green Monster, but it feels like it's right over that horizon. That atmosphere sets you up for Fenway. When you finally get to Fenway, it will be like Portland—except times a thousand.

When I told my family I was going to Portland, Maine, they didn't even know where that was. The city is awesome—I'd still go on a vacation there. I always say that Portland and Pawtucket are the two best places to play minor-league ball. In Portland, the fans treated us great. The little kids knew who we were—I mean, we were on the Sea Dogs, and kids were yelling to me, "Dustin! Dustin!"

I was playing well right from the start. At one point I was leading the league in hitting, at something like .331. Todd Claus was my manager again. He'd moved up to Portland with all of us, and after games he would post all the stats for the league. When I went over and had a look, I saw that I was first in hits, first in average, and first in runs.

Ben Cherington showed up one time, and he was smiling.

He said, "Man, I didn't think you were going to do this well this early."

And I said, "Well, what the f— did you think I was going to do?" He just laughed. I think he and I started building a relationship then. I think he saw that I was pretty much about one thing, which was helping whatever team I was on win. That was my job. I said, "My personality isn't just that I play to win, it's that I have to try to help everybody else out, because this game sucks—it's not easy, it's tough. I want to be a guy who helps my teammates find the best they have, too."

As I was telling this to Ben, he was laughing. I was just a kid, and he thought I was hilarious.

THAT SUMMER, WE had real fun in Portland. We had Lester there, and Pap. Kason Gabbard was there, Murph, Brandon Moss—most of that team is in the big leagues now. We were coming up together. We were winning games. And the organization was noticing.

At the beginning of May, one of our pitchers, Cla Meredith, got called up to Triple A, threw one inning, then went up to the big leagues. I thought, Dude, I can smell this shit, it's coming . . . Boston was just a couple of hours down the road, and as I said, Portland was a place where you could get a sense of the intensity that surrounds everything about the Red Sox.

Just as he did at Sarasota, Todd Claus told us not to worry about getting to Boston. He said to worry about winning games in the Eastern League. That would take the pressure off, and the rest would take care of itself.

"You play for the Sea Dogs," he said. "You aren't the Red Sox yet." He said that if we kept on winning, the people in Boston were going to want to have a look. He said if you play hard and you're good, you'll keep moving up. Everybody knew the key was to stick to doing your own job as well as you possibly could.

Sure enough, in midseason I got the call to go to the next level. I was being brought up to Triple A. I'd played sixty-six games in Portland, and had hit .324. I was on the move again.

IT WASN'T EXACTLY a setback when I got to Pawtucket, but it was different. The fun of the low minors was that everybody was young, twenty or twenty-one or twenty-two, getting a feel for playing professional baseball and still excited about even being paid to play.

Now I was in Triple A. I was playing with thirty-year-old guys, and some of them had already been in the big leagues and were here to try to get back up. Shawn Wooten was there, and he'd won a World Series with the Angels in 2002. Dave Berg was there, and he'd played for the Marlins and the Blue Jays—these were veterans.

In Triple A, winning isn't exactly the priority. Guys are going up and down to and from the major leagues. If the major-league team needs some quick help, they go grab somebody from Triple A. There is a bit of development for young players, but mainly it's keeping older guys ready to go, one step away from the majors. It's like you're already pretty much there, and just waiting to get that phone call.

In Pawtucket, they did everything first-class. The owner was Ben Mondor, who was eighty years old and had bought the team back in the 1970s. He made it a great situation. One time we all went out on a yacht and had a big lobster dinner down in Newport. He treated everybody great—but it wasn't just Ben, it was everybody who worked for the team. I made a lot of friends playing there.

The Pawtucket Red Sox play at McCoy Stadium, which has ten thousand seats. It was full for almost every home game I played there. It was feeling closer and closer to being big-league.

It was easy to get wrapped up watching guys go up and down to and from the major leagues, but you don't want to be that guy. You want to be a guy who goes up and *stays* up. There's a lot of labeling that goes on in Triple A, and it can be easy to get stuck in what people think you are.

It started off great. The first four games, I was hitting something like .413. I was *raking*.

And up in Boston, the second baseman, Mark Bellhorn, was struggling with an injury. Fenway Park was only forty-five miles away now. I was just trying to play hard and waiting for something to happen.

And then something did. But not what I had hoped. On June 25, 2005, my sixth game for the PawSox, I got up to bat in the first inning with a man on first. My job was to move him over. I was trying to push bunt, for God's sake. I got hit in the hand.

As soon as it hit me, I knew it wasn't good. I thought I'd broken it. My hand swelled up immediately.

It messed me up. I'd never been hurt on a baseball field since I'd been hit in the face. The doctor said it was going take at least two or three weeks to heal, and that I was just going to have to deal with it. But I didn't want to sit out.

Then the thirty-year-old guys started getting on me. They were saying, "Hey, what's the matter with you? Why aren't you playing? Are you not tough?"

They said, "Are you soft or something?"

Now that's the exact opposite of the way I am. I tried to play, of course, and I didn't tell manager Ron Johnson—R. J.—how bad it was. It was my left hand, so I could still throw.

I tried to play, and it wasn't going very well. The next five games, I don't even think I got a hit. R. J. obviously knew something was up. I wasn't hitting the ball with any pop, and I just wasn't myself. So he came up to me on an overnight bus trip.

"Hey, kid, how're you doing?"

"Great, R. J. What's up?"

He said, "I just wanted to thank you for the effort you're putting out. I know it's tough to start with the injury. Put 'er there." And he put out his hand to shake my hand. And then he grabbed my injured hand, and he just crushed it. When he gripped it, I crumpled to the floor of the bus.

He said, "You're done for a month."

I thought, Oh, shit. They found out.

But the fact was, my hand was killing me. I'd tried to play through it, and I couldn't.

In Boston, Bellhorn went on the disabled list, and the Red Sox needed a second baseman. They ended up trading for Tony Graffanino, and he finished the season at second base.

I understood how it worked. I was still hoping to get called up in September, but it didn't happen then, either. They called up other guys, including Hanley Ramirez. My season was all over.

I just had to say to myself, "You know how it works, and you have to pay your dues. I'm just going to make sure that next year I come in ready to go."

That was the 2005 season, which had started out so great and ended with some frustration. And, to make matters worse, in the last game of the season I got into a collision with a first baseman in Ottawa, and my knee just blew up. I couldn't do much. When I got back home it was hurting so bad I had to get it checked out by the doctors in the offseason.

Ron Johnson

Manager, Pawtucket Red Sox

Dustin played for me in Pawtucket in 2005 and 2006.

The thing about Pedey when he first came to play for me: obviously you look at his stature and it puts a doubt in your mind and that's not a negative. You've been conditioned as an evaluator and a coach to look at the six-foot-two, 195-pound specimen and project him. You don't look at Pedey that way. The first time I saw him during spring training was at minicamp.

I was asking people, "Where's Pedroia?"

"That's Pedroia," someone said, and pointed him out.

I looked over. He's got his hat down over his eyes and he's got this big-ass swing in the cage and he's not a large man and he's not extremely fast. He's faster now than he was then. He runs better and is in phenomenal shape. But the hardest thing that you can't evaluate, that obviously our front office did, was the heart and desire and the actual baseball skills, overlooking the height and strength. They were able to look at a guy who does nothing but put the barrel to the baseball. They looked at the swing and the way he played.

Even when we had him at Triple A, no one was sure. We were moving him over to shortstop and playing him at third. You're looking at him thinking, Well, does he have enough arm to play over there?

To me he's a tremendous inspirational poster boy for any kid who wants to play in the big leagues. His whole life, he's always been the guy people thought wasn't going to be that good. Obviously what he's proved to the baseball world is he's one of the best players in the game.

I would love to sit here and tell Pedey, "Yeah, I knew you would be the MVP of the American League." But I didn't.

Of course, he did and you can't overlook that. There's no doubt in my mind now, that even when he was in Pawtucket he knew the American League Rookie of the Year award was waiting for him. He knew the MVP award was waiting for him.

He was probably thinking, Who wouldn't vote for me?

And you know what? He was right. I'm a believer. I'd get in a foxhole with him.

There are so many stories with Pedey. Every day with him is an experience. But there's one story and this one is beautiful.

Chris Wilson was pitching for the Yankees Triple-A team and David Pauley had started for us. David hit something like six guys in that one game. He hit three or four of them with curveballs and some were in the head. It was one of those games where we were getting the shit beat out of us.

About the seventh inning, we knew it was Wilson's last inning. He had pitched in the big leagues, with Kansas City. He was carving us up. There was no bad blood going on, but I was waiting for it. I was waiting for retaliation.

I was thinking, We've hit six guys and a veteran pitcher is going to show his team he's got their back...They knew that when Pauley hit them, it was never intentional, but it was just the fact we hit so many of their guys.

Sure enough, I'm looking at it and there are two outs and here's Pedroia coming to the plate in the seventh inning.

I was wondering if they would, with him in there. First fastball was away, but the second fastball was right in the thigh.

They got him. Pedey was going crazy.

He was screaming, "Son of a bitch, we're going to make this right! That's bullshit!"

Ken Huckaby was our catcher and he was yelling and screaming, too.

I walked over to Pedey and said, "Hey, do you know that we've hit six of their guys tonight?"

All of a sudden he was like, "Really?"

I said, "Yeah. Six. What just happened was pretty professional to me. It's unfortunate it was you who got hit, but we've hit three in the head and three others. That's six. The guy just sent a statement."

Pedey said, "Oh! I didn't realize that."

Then he just ran out to his position.

It was beautiful.

Right when he arrived halfway through the 2005 season, he was having a good year. You knew it was inevitable that he was going to get a call to the big leagues.

Red Sox second baseman Mark Bellhorn had gotten hurt and we were on a trip, I think it was Canada because we were in that dead-communication zone on the bus when you're coming down the back way. We had stopped and I got a call from the group—it was Ben Cherington and Theo Epstein and all those guys. They were leaning toward calling Pedey up to the big leagues. You could tell they were waiting to hear the right word.

Pedey was saying his hand was kind of so-so, that it wasn't bothering him that much. He came back a little early and played a little bit but he just didn't have that pop in the bat. I'll never forget it because Theo and Ben were going on and on and they really needed to know if Pedey was hurt or not.

I said, "Well, let me do some investigating."

Pedey was on my bus and there was only one thing I could think of to figure out if he was hurting. So I went in the back of the bus like I was going to the bathroom. Guys were playing cards and stuff and he was sitting there.

I said, "Hey, Pedey, what's up, man?" We started talking.

Then I grabbed his hand, and he buckled.

I said sarcastically, "Oh, really? You're not hurt?"

I went back to the front of the bus. We made another stop and I was able to get reception so I plugged my phone in to get a signal.

I called them back and said, "Nope, he's not your guy right now."

It would be another full year before he'd get the call to the major leagues.

I don't think he ever knew how close he was that time.

8

The Winds of Change

In the off-season before the 2006 season, a couple of things happened that were going to change things.

First, on November 21, 2005, the Red Sox acquired Josh Beckett from the Florida Marlins. To get him, the Red Sox traded away Hanley Ramirez, which was a surprise. Hanley had always seemed like the shortstop of the future for the Red Sox. People had talked about him as being the top prospect in the organization. And now he was gone. The Red Sox also took on another player in the deal, third baseman Mike Lowell.

Then, in December, the Red Sox traded Doug Mirabelli for second baseman Mark Loretta. It was pretty clear he was going to be the starting second baseman for the Red Sox. But the media were saying he was probably going to be a one-year member of the team, because his contract was up at the end of the year and he was thirty-four years old.

I tried to focus on working hard to prepare myself. Hanley's situation showed you can never know what's going to happen, but you always want to be ready for opportunities that come to you. Hanley would end up being the National League Rookie of the Year in 2006.

I was letting my hand heal and trying to deal with my knee. I felt like things had gone well, but I knew I was looking at Pawtucket when the 2006 season came. I wanted to do what I could to play at my best.

It was good to reflect on the season. And it was good to spend time with Kelli after that hectic 2005. She had come to be with me right after I'd hurt my hand, but during the season there's a lot going on. Now we could just be quiet and hang out and enjoy being with each other. It had been a year since we had met, but our relationship had become very serious.

We got engaged that winter. I actually called her dad, Brad Hatley, up in Chicago. He's a really nice guy. The Hatleys are laid-back midwesterners. I just asked him, "Is it all right that I ask your daughter to marry me?"

He said, "Yeah, no problem. Just one thing: you'll have to take me to California for some deep-sea fishing."

I was like, "Shit. No problem, man. That's pretty damn easy. I thought you were going to yell at me and tell me I couldn't do all this stuff."

He was awesome. I think he was just joking, but I did end up taking him deep-sea fishing this past off-season. It was a great trip.

Kelli's mom, Jennie, was very excited, too.

Kelli and I went up to a place called the Boulders, in Arizona north of Phoenix. I got us a nice suite and we went out to dinner, eight courses. It was really nice, and something neither of us was used to.

I had arranged to have the hotel put loads of flowers in our room. With a spa setup, there was romantic stuff everywhere. And then I asked her.

It was fun, and I think she was also excited to see the romantic side of Dustin Pedroia. Seriously, I'm a real pimp.

Kelli Pedroia

It didn't faze me at all, when I met Dustin, that he was a baseball player. I never followed baseball, although my brother, Brandon, played football, basketball, and baseball, and my parents always followed sports. But pretty quickly, I learned how crazy he was about the game.

When I met him in the fall of 2004, he was playing in the Arizona Fall League, and I was in my senior year at Arizona State. Everyone called him Pedro then. When we first met, I set him up with one of my roommates. There was a formal, and I said to her, "Why don't you ask Pedro to take you?" They went together, but then I thought, Why am I setting him up with other girls? I had liked him as soon as I met him.

He was actually a little shy at first.

We really connected with each other a couple of weeks later, on Halloween. There was a party at a bar, and I saw him there. I was dressed as a cowgirl. He went to the party as an OB/GYN. You get the picture. We've been partners in crime ever since.

That night, we really talked to each other and had so much fun.

I know this sounds funny, but we knew that night that it was love at first sight. Two weeks after we started seeing each other, we were telling people that we were going to get married. We knew it that soon. We got engaged a year later.

It was a whirlwind. I knew that as a minor-league baseball player, he didn't know where he'd be the following season, but over that winter we were really able to get to know each other. By the time he left for spring training, we knew we would continue to be together.

My parents are such good, easygoing people. They liked Dustin immediately and saw how good a person Dustin is, and how good he is to me. My family lives in Chicago, and my brother is a die-hard Cubs fan, so he and Dustin give each other trouble about that. When Dustin asked me to marry him, he first asked for my parents' permission, and that meant a lot to them.

During the beginning of the 2005 season, I was getting ready to graduate from Arizona State, and we'd see each other once a month. He was playing in Portland, Maine. Then he was called up to the Pawtucket Red Sox. Our plan was that I was going to come out and stay with him there for the rest of the season. The night before I flew out to join him, he hurt his hand.

I saw how Triple A can be hard on the players. You're one at-bat away from the major leagues, or one injury away. When I flew in, I could see how much pain Dustin was in. It was really bad. But he didn't want to tell anybody. He'd go out and play and try not to let on how much it was affecting him. But when he was at home, I could see it.

Ron Johnson, the PawSox manager, was able to figure out that Dustin's injury was worse than he was letting on. Once he did, the

Red Sox had Dustin go up to Boston to have an MRI on his hand. It was such a difficult time for Dustin. He really felt that he was playing well enough to get a chance to get called up, but then this had happened.

On the way into Boston we got stuck in the worst traffic jam you could imagine. Everybody was crawling along, and we wondered if there had been a bad accident or something awful like that. But little by little, we figured it out. People had on Red Sox hats and T-shirts. We realized we were stuck in all the traffic going to the Red Sox game. Dustin was already hurting enough, and disappointed that he wasn't able to play.

But then Dustin smiled and pointed for me to see something.

"There it is," he said.

I saw the light towers.

"That's Fenway Park over there," he said. "We're going to be there next year."

That was all he said. He wasn't hoping it, or boasting about it, he was just saying it. I could see him looking over there at Fenway Park as we rolled slowly by. I thought about how that might be, that someday there might be people who would be willing to put up with a traffic jam on the way to Fenway Park to go see Dustin Pedroia play.

9

Going to the Show

Spring training in 2006 was different than the year before. In 2005, I'd set my sights on playing for the Sea Dogs, but now I was looking to get myself ready to try to make the big step to the majors. It was an experience, being around the big-league camp. Here were all these guys I'd heard all about. David Ortiz and Josh Beckett and Jason Varitek and, of course, Manny Ramirez.

Because of the knee injury, I came into 2006 overweight. I was 190 pounds. I was huge. I was fat. I couldn't run, because they'd told me not to.

But I was in my first big-league camp. And the first swing I took, my shoulder popped out of its socket. I was like, "What the hell's going on with me?"

It had been a combination of things. I was out of shape, and maybe because of that I took an awkward swing, and now my shoulder had popped out. If you're in shape, that kind of thing doesn't happen. But I couldn't get in shape, because my knee was hurt. Now it was a lose-lose situation.

I rehabbed my shoulder for six weeks, and any chance I had of showing the Red Sox what I could do didn't happen.

I started the 2006 season a week late in Pawtucket. After the first fifty at-bats, I was hitting .230.

I was miserable, and everybody around me was, too. Triple A can be an awful place because it's easy to get bitter that you're not in the big leagues. It's fun, but it's not fun. It's great that you're just a step away, but it sucks that you're just a step away. You don't want to be there.

I remember sitting at home, and I'm thinking, This isn't me, to be like this. I'm not a .230 hitter. Are you kidding me?

I knew I had to do better. I didn't want to be just another one of those guys who's up and down, up and down—or be a guy who stays in Triple A and never gets his shot.

Maybe that's what did it. I went on a streak like I'd never been on in my life. I went from .230 after 260 at-bats to .321 in something like 340 at-bats. It was an eighty-at-bat streak, like I might have been 60 for 80.

I mean, I unleashed the fury of line drives all over McCoy Stadium. It was *awesome.* It was, "It's Free Welding Goggles Night at McCoy Stadium, and come see the free Pedroia Laser Show, too!"

That was happening as my shoulder began healing, my knee was improving, and I was getting healthy.

I was hitting .320 and it was August, and I began to think, My time is coming. I knew the Red Sox were expanding the roster in September, and the fans were putting on some pressure to bring me up. I knew something had to happen. That's how it was in Boston. If I were someplace else, like with the Milwaukee Brewers, the fans probably would have said to leave me down there and not start the clock for arbitration, or something like that. But this was Boston.

The weekend of August 19 and 20, we were playing in Ottawa, Ontario, against the Lynx. What a dump that place was! The city's nice, and the field wasn't bad, but the clubhouse! It's like they'd burnt that place down or something. And the weather was unbelievable. It was August, but it felt like it was about 20 degrees. Did they even *have* summer?

That night, I looked at the lineup card, and for the first game I was going to be the designated hitter. That hadn't happened before. Weird. I looked at that card and I thought, I'm going to be the baddest DH on the planet Earth! But still, I had no idea what was going on. Clausy had done that once in a while in Double A; there was one time where we had three doubleheaders in a row in Portland, because it had snowed so much, and I had DH'd all of them, because I never missed a game all the time I was there. I figured R. J. was doing that just to give me a break.

So that night I DH'd, but then R. J. took me out after my second at-bat.

I said to myself, "What's up? I haven't done anything stupid, I don't think . . ." But I hadn't been taken out of a game in a long time. I thought, He can't be punishing me, can he? So what's the deal?

R. J. didn't say anything to me. I said, "R. J., what the hell's going on?"

He said, "Hey kid, just sit down and relax."

I said, "Whatever." But I was sitting there on the bench, and now we were getting our asses kicked on the field. It was bothering me. I was sitting there thinking, What the hell?

In the next game, Abe Alvarez was pitching, and he was just shoving. It's like 1-0 in fifteen minutes, and he was throwing a great game, and here I was not playing. I was thinking they were punishing me for not doing something, but I didn't know what. I kept running the possibilities through my head: I mean, they'd told me they didn't want me sliding into bases headfirst, and I'd keep doing it and they'd yell at me and fine me a hundred bucks. Because of my shoulder, they didn't want me doing that. But sometimes I didn't care.

But now I was sitting there on the bench thinking, Wait a minute. I haven't slid headfirst in a while . . .

Then R. J. called me over and said, "Hey kid, you're going to the big leagues."

I said, "You couldn't have told me that in the last four innings? I've been sitting there on my ass wondering what was going on! I thought I was in trouble this whole time!"

He said, "No, you're all right. You're flying out of Ottawa at six A.M. and you're meeting the team in Anaheim." He told me to take a shower and get changed. He shook my hand, this time for real.

Over that weekend, the Red Sox had just been swept five games at Fenway by the Yankees. I said to myself, "If they think I'm going to be the savior, I have news for them . . ." I didn't fully know what the hell I was doing . . . I mean, I was in *Ottawa*.

It had been a three-day trip up, so I hadn't packed a lot. I didn't even have my suit there. Usually, they have you bring a suit in case you get called up. But I hadn't even brought it. I called Kelli and said, "Kelli, get my suit and fly to Anaheim with it."

She said, "Why?"

I said, "Because I just got called up."

She was really excited. She was in Chicago planning our wedding. She bought me a suit that wasn't going to fit exactly, and went to the airport and got on a plane for California.

I called my parents, and they jumped right in the car to make the six-hour drive to Anaheim. They were going crazy.

It was a long flight, and quiet, and I did a lot of thinking. I was thinking that *this was it*. I didn't want to just be excited about being called up for a game. I wanted to be thinking about the longer haul. I was telling myself that I was going to go up to the big leagues, and I was going to stay in the big leagues for twenty years. I had just turned twenty-three, and on that flight to Anaheim, I decided that they were never going to get me out of a Boston Red Sox uniform.

Steve Hyder

Radio Play-by-Play Announcer

Pawtucket Red Sox

For me it's remarkable to be around the game. I grew up a Red Sox fan, so to have a front-row seat to watch guys—and this is my sixth year with the PawSox—you look at the list and see who has played here before moving on to Boston: Pedroia and Youkilis and Papelbon and Lester and Lowrie and Ellsbury. The list goes on and on.

Knowing these guys before they become stars is really something. We spend more time together than we do with our own families. With these kids . . . I started out and I was more the players' age, but after being here a while, now I'm more the age of the management.

You get close during the season with a lot of the players. Most of them are really nice kids, and quiet. They're waiting. They're hoping.

There was something different about Pedey right away. There was this air of confidence about him. If you weren't on his side, I guess you might call it arrogance, but there's this lovability about him. He walks in the room acting like he's six foot four and 225 pounds and that he looks like Brad Pitt, but for some reason you find it endearing instead of irritating.

Pedroia loved to complain. It was all good-natured. His daily greeting to me was, "Hyder, what the f—?"

I'd say, "What's the matter today, Pedey?"

It was always something. "This team's field is terrible" or "The weather sucks today" or whatever. He loved to talk. He was almost like a little brother, bugging you and making noise.

Then you see him play. You say, "This guy has no business doing this well." It's like he's willed himself into being such a great player.

I've seen guys in Triple A who play hard, play well, and just sit there waiting for a call that never comes. Back in 2004, Tim Kester was the PawSox Pitcher of the Year, but he was being used as a starter, and the Red Sox didn't need a starter. If he'd been used as a reliever, he might have been a guy who got the call. He had the stuff to be a major-league pitcher, but it never happened. There was a guy named Bobby Scales, who batted right at .300 for the last three seasons in Triple A but never got called up, and now he's thirty, wondering. He's got all the tools and all the ability, but he never got that break. He's been in the minors for ten seasons. There are guys who are down on the depth chart on one team who, if they played for another organization, could be playing in the major leagues every day. There's a lot of waiting.

I've always felt the waiting. Every major-league team has twenty-five roster spots, and every team has two radio guys. I always say it's harder to make it to the big leagues as a radio guy than as a player. So we're all waiting our turn, waiting for something to happen. You ride the buses with the players, you stay in the crummy hotels, you eat the fast food, you're making those 2 A.M. stops on the New York State Thruway to grab some junk food—and you know that for the chosen few, once they've hit it big, their lives change in a huge way. It's remarkable to see people have an incredible dream really come true. It's not that you have anything to do with them having their success, but you get to know them and you can't help but be thrilled for the ones who get the call. You also can't help but be saddened for all the ones who get so close, then never see it happen.

That summer of 2006, the PawSox were on a road trip playing the Ottawa Lynx. It was an absolutely horrible day—cold and raining. That place, Lynx Stadium, it was like a mausoleum—they've since shut down operations due to lack of fan support.

My radio partner, Dan Hoard, and I were up in that tiny press box they had there, and we had heard the rumbling that Pedroia might be getting the call to the majors at some point. That night, he left the game and during a commercial break I said to Dan, "I'm going down to see what the story is." I wanted to make sure that if he was leaving—because a lot of times they have to leave right away—I could do an interview and get a reaction from him about what it feels like to make the Show.

I went down into the bowels of Lynx Stadium, and looked for Dustin in the clubhouse. He wasn't there. I peeked into the dugout, which is kind of off-limits during a ball game, but I guess because I was part of the traveling entourage I was given a certain amount of leeway.

I got Dustin to look over, and I motioned to him, and said, "What's up?"

He said, "Nothing." But he had a smile on his face. It was unspoken, but I picked up the drift that he knew he was getting the call.

I went back up to the booth, and then after the game we finished up our broadcast and I went back down to the clubhouse. The place was cleared out. The players were all on the bus, ready to go. One guy was going to the major leagues that night, and the rest of them were getting on a bus late at night for a long ride home, back home to wait.

But then Dustin came out of the shower. He was standing there, soaking wet and with no clothes on, and I asked him what was up.

He said, "I got the call."

I said, "Oh my God! Congratulations!" And in about the most spontaneous way I've ever seen, he came at me and gave me a bear hug. He was so happy. All the years of playing and now it had happened.

All of a sudden he realized he was stark naked and soaking wet and he jumped back and we both sort of went, "Whoa!"

We both had a laugh. It was just his genuine, unbridled, tremendous joy.

That's how I remember Dustin Pedroia becoming a major leaguer.

10

Batter Up

My parents got into Anaheim just as my flight came in, so they drove over and picked me up at the airport. Then Kelli got in about an hour later. We all rode to the ballpark together.

I was in California, and I was tired, going on two hours of sleep. I went to the field straight from the airport. I sat there for five hours, waiting. Then Tito showed up.

He said, "Hey, kid, what's going on?" He told me he was excited to see me play, and that I was going to bat ninth that night and play shortstop.

I called him "Coach" and he yelled at me. "Call me Terry!" he shouted.

"Okay . . . Terry . . ."

"So have fun," he said.

And that was it. I said, "Hey, easy enough."

IN THE TOP of the second inning, I got my first big-league at-bat. The bases were loaded with one out, with no score. Joe

Saunders was pitching. I hit a line drive, but the Angels' shortstop, Orlando Cabrera, got to it and then tagged second to double up Mike Lowell.

I came up again in the fourth with two out and nobody on. Saunders was still pitching, and I got hold of one for a line drive to center field for my first major-league hit. I stood on first base and thought, Okay, now I have that out of the way. It was good to get a hit in my first game. It was cool.

In the ninth, with us behind by one run, they had Manny Ramirez pinch-hit for me, and I even thought that was cool. Most times, when they put in a pinch hitter for you, you're pissed. But I'm thinking, Manny Ramirez, pinch-hitting for *me*. He had a better chance than me of going long. He flied out, though, and we lost 4-3.

MY FIRST GAME at Fenway Park was the last day of August 2006, against the Blue Jays. I was only hitting .138 after nine games in the major leagues, and I sat down in the clubhouse to get dressed and wondered if the fans were going to boo me. But when I got out there on the field, they didn't boo me. They seemed to want to see a homegrown guy do well. Any team takes a certain amount of risk when they draft a player and work to bring him up through the system, and I think everybody wanted that to work. I don't remember much about that first game at Fenway; we won and I didn't get a hit.

FOR THE REST of the 2006 season, I felt like I hit the ball well, but I didn't have much luck.

Still, being on the field at Fenway Park was an amazing experience.

Every day that you show up at Fenway is exciting. There isn't a day that goes by that you're out of the pennant race. There's never a day when the fans aren't going to show up until the fourth inning or leave after seven; the fans are there by the time batting practice starts, and they're ready to go.

On the field, it surrounds you: You see the signs, and you smell the food cooking—the hot dogs and the popcorn and all the other stuff. You smell baseball when you're standing out there at the edge of the infield.

I love when the fans say they love the smell of hot dogs and all that, but as a player my biggest thing is to smell the grass. You go out there and it's just different, especially when you first get to spring training. You're out there early in the morning and the grass is still wet and you can smell it.

It just feels like baseball. When I'd walk out onto the field at Fenway and the grass was cut, it brought me to that, how baseball feels when it feels right. You don't have a care in the world once you step onto that field. The only thing you're trying to do is play baseball. It's fun.

As a player, what more can you ask for? Fenway Park has the greatest baseball atmosphere I've ever seen. We go on road trips, and there's no other stadium that compares to what goes on at Fenway. The Boston fans love their team. They care about one thing: the Red Sox winning. It's unbelievable to have that support behind you. It can also be tough when it's not there.

I only had eighty-nine at-bats with the Red Sox by the end of 2006. I hit a lot of shots that ended up getting caught. I hit a couple of home runs, but with so few at-bats, every one of them mattered. If I'd had seven more hits, I'd have gone from hitting .190 to .270, and people would have spent the off-season thinking I was great. But I didn't. I hit .190, and that was the bottom line.

I WENT INTO the off-season not knowing what to expect. In 2006 they had gotten Mark Loretta for one year to play second base, and so I was wondering if that was waiting for me next. I sensed it was my spot to earn in 2007.

At the end of the 2006 season, Theo sat me down and said, "Look, if you come into next season in the best shape you've ever been in your life—you get faster, you get stronger, everything—it's your job. We're counting on you and we know what you can do."

I thought, Either you're an idiot, or you're the first guy who ever came at it that way. My whole life, the only people who believed in me were my parents. Everyone else, even my high school coach, were people I had to make into believers. I'd turned them into believers at the minor-league level, but no one had ever seen what I could do at this level. And this was the highest level you could go to.

So I started working out, and returned to Athletes' Performance in Arizona.

When the Sox told me to get into the best shape of my life, I knew what I had to do. I needed to lose weight. I needed to strengthen my core. I've always been a strong guy, but it was awkwardly strong—baseball strong. It wasn't as if I could lift a couch or something. I could hit a home run, even though I'm not a very big guy. You could say that was a little bit freakish.

I started working out and dieting to the point where I wouldn't even put a piece of gum in my mouth, because I didn't want to deal with that one calorie. It was advanced training until I couldn't even stand up.

I also got married that off-season. It was in Chicago, on November 11, right after the season ended. It was a great day. Kelli looked beautiful and both our families did things up nicely. And some of my oldest friends were there to be part of it.

My best man, Zeb Vigil, was one of my best friends in middle school. We had every class together in seventh, eighth, and ninth grades. Once we got to ninth grade we could play freshman football, and he was the center. He's a huge guy, probably six feet, three inches tall, 280 to 300 pounds.

I was the quarterback, and told him, "Zeb, make sure I don't get killed. I weigh a hundred and ten pounds, dude." We were running the option and all this stuff and he said, "All right, man, I'll make sure no one hits you." But, sure enough, I ended up breaking my leg. In the next game, Zeb hurt his neck really badly. He had to have a neck brace, and I was in a wheelchair with a cast up to my hip. So there we were, a couple of thirteen-year-olds, him in his brace pushing me in my wheelchair to every class. Joey Nolan was another one of my best friends and lived down the street. Bobby Hawke played baseball with me. Jared Hunter. They were quality guys growing up in a small town, like I was. We really didn't do much except play sports. That's all we cared about.

Zeb liked the A's and I liked the Giants, and so we would get into it. Jared liked the 49ers, as I did, and the other guys liked the Raiders, so there was always a friendly competition with everybody. That's what makes friendships special. I could joke around with these guys when I was a young kid, and still do today. We stay in touch and they usually come out to Boston once a year to see me play and get together.

KELLI AND I honeymooned in Hawaii, on Maui. I'd get up at six in the morning and run on the treadmill for thirty minutes. We'd do stuff all day, and when we came back in the evening, around nine o'clock, I ran for thirty more minutes on the treadmill. Even on my honeymoon I was possessed.

When we returned to Arizona, it was right to Athletes' Performance. I'd get there at seven in the morning, eat breakfast, then get right into my speed and agility work. I'd drink a protein shake, then hit and throw. I'd come back and eat lunch. Then I'd lift weights all afternoon. I'd come home and Kelli would cook me dinner, and then after dinner I'd go out and run again. It was like that for six weeks. She must have thought she had just married a maniac.

I started to lose weight. I began to lean up. My pants got too big, and I told her I had to get a new pair of jeans.

She said, "Why do you need new pants?"

"I need pants because I'm totally jacked."

It was awesome. I was working my ass off, and feeling like I was going to have a year I'd never forget. This was my time. Screw everybody else. I'd earned this shit.

I came into spring training in 2007 weighing 170 pounds. I'd lost twenty-three pounds. I had 12 percent body fat, and I'd never been under 15 percent in my life. I've always been short and stocky, and it was hard getting down to 12 percent.

I felt good. I felt ready.

Terry Francona

Manager

Boston Red Sox

My first recollection of Dustin is of him coming into camp his first spring. He was a little shorter than I expected, although I had been forewarned not to let first impressions matter, because this kid could play.

But my first impression was that he was kind of fat: short and dumpy.

Then he got hurt his first at-bat of spring training. We were over playing Minnesota [at Hammond Stadium in Lee County] and he took a swing and threw his shoulder out of place, and that was it.

Now that he's two years removed from that, it seems kind of funny. But I don't know how funny it was at the time. He didn't get to do much because he mostly sat in the trainer's room and worked on his shoulder.

It's easy to fall in love with him as a player because you can trust him. I mean, he doesn't have to hit .350 or be the MVP, but he's going to give you every ounce and everything he has to try to win. And when someone does that, it's all you can ask.

He shows up every day and he wants to win. When he comes into the room, the room gets brighter. He's upbeat. He's good. He's accountable. He's conscientious. Shit, you put a good adjective there and I'll put [his] name next to it.

All those things you hear is what makes him Pedey. He lacks no confidence, and he shouldn't. I remember in 2008 when we were in the middle of interleague play in June, and we went through Houston and he was hitting 0-fer. He was probably hitting about .250 and he was miserable. He just felt like he was letting everybody down.

It's funny, but I was real careful about what to say to him, because even with the great relationship we had developed, I didn't want him to think we were panicking, because we weren't. He would walk in the door and I would say, "Pedey, it's going to be okay."

He'd say, "I know."

I didn't want him to think we were worried about him.

We have a lot in common. He loves cribbage. So do I. We have ten or twelve guys on our team who play cribbage. I do this with a lot of guys. Tim Wakefield and I play the day Wake pitches. It's just kind of a ritual.

With Pedey, we'll get that one game of cribbage in on each game day, and we'll talk a little shit. Sometimes it's a serious conversation, but more often than not it's not. People don't understand, but we're there all day so it's not like you can put your game face on at one-thirty in the afternoon and put your spikes on. There's a lot of time to sit around and talk and kind of BS and be a regular person. I enjoy that.

Baseball players are routine oriented and he's no different. He gets there earlier than almost anybody else. I think he likes to get his lifting out of the way, so he just has time to be a teammate. He sits around and talks a lot of shit at people. He just sits at his locker and waits for people to come wandering in and he just attacks them. And more often than not, he just gets crushed right back. He has that unique personality where he'll start talking shit and about halfway through he'll kind of laugh and say, "Yeah, I know."

He's very true to himself. He's very sincere and he comes across that way. Some of the things he says, you wouldn't be able to get away with it, but it's him. Guys love him. He's kind of the little brother. You can beat on him, but no one else better beat on him.

Even when he's not hitting, you know you're going to get more than his numbers. You're going to get a good defensive play late in the game. You're going to get the ability to steal a base with the game on the line. He's just always trying to find a way to be better than the other team.

He's the kind of guy who, when he wakes up in the morning, gets out of bed wanting to kick somebody's ass . . .

11

Rough Start

Spring training in 2007 was a madhouse. We'd signed Japanese pitcher Daisuke Matsuzaka, better known as Dice-K. Everybody wanted to see this guy, and there were a billion pictures of him all over the place, as if he were Elvis Presley. This atmosphere, this craziness, it's the Boston thing, the Red Sox thing, with people lined up to watch spring training games and the media all over the place.

I got to choose my number for the year.

I had been number 64 for that last part of the 2006 season, but in the beginning of 2007, it was either 3 or 15. I didn't want to be 3 because even though Jimmie Foxx had worn it back in the thirties and forties, Mark Loretta had just worn 3, and Edgar Renteria before him. So I took number 15. The last player who wore 15, Kevin Millar, was a clown. I love that guy. Millar is awesome and every time we play against him, I tell him, "Dude, I'm the real one-five."

It's just to keep it fun. But there was nothing significant behind wearing number 15.

I'd had my time with the team at the end of 2006, so I felt a little more familiar coming back to spring training. Most of the guys were very welcoming as I came back in. There's a funny story, though, involving Manny Ramirez.

I had first met Manny when I was in minor-league camp that first spring training, in 2005. I went with one of my roommates to Best Buy and Manny was there by himself. He was buying some CDs. I went over to him and introduced myself. I said, "Hey, I just got drafted by the Red Sox and I wanted to say hello."

I had always been a big Manny fan. We stood there in the Best Buy and I talked to him then, and he was great. I didn't see him again for the rest of 2005. And I didn't talk to him that much when I got called up in 2006. I was a new guy, and knew my place, and Manny was just doing his thing.

I came back for camp in 2007, and something hilarious happened. Manny had run into my wife—we lived down the street from Manny in spring training in Cape Coral that year—at the gas station. My wife, who is very friendly and outgoing, went up to him and said, "Hi, Manny. I'm Dustin Pedroia's wife. I just wanted to introduce myself."

This was going into 2007 and there was a pretty good chance I was going to be the starting second baseman, so we were getting to know everyone. Kelli told me about meeting Manny, and how nice he was to her, and how she was so excited to be treated the way he treated her. I got to the ballpark the next day and went into the outfield and said to him, "Hey, Manny, I heard you met my wife at the gas station in Cape Coral."

He said, "No. I didn't meet your wife. I met Pedey's wife."

I said, "No, Manny, that's my wife."

He said, "No. No. That's Pedey's wife!"

I said, "Manny, what the f—? I *am* Pedey! What the hell is wrong with you?" I was arguing with Manny Ramirez over whether I was me. He almost had me believing I wasn't.

At the start of the season, I didn't think he even knew who the hell I was. I didn't know what was going on. After that it was kind of weird. I told some of the guys and they said, "Dude, listen. He really doesn't know you yet. When he gets to know you he'll remember your name and shit like that."

"Oh, okay. That sounds good."

IN SPRING TRAINING, I got five hits, total. I'd come in after hitting .190 in 2006 and only got five hits in all of spring training. People were looking at this and saying, "Can this guy possibly be any good?"

I was thinking, No shit. I'm not a dumbass. I know what you're thinking. I knew I was good, but I also knew I hadn't done it yet. I was waiting for the time it was going to happen, because I knew it was coming. I could *feel* it.

Toward the end of spring training I went into my meeting with Theo. I was sitting there with my five hits—I've never really been a good spring training player. Luckily, they don't count the hits you get in spring training, they count the ones you get in the season.

Theo said, "Listen: I don't care if you hit .150, your job is to help this team win. I don't care if you have to go out there and play like an absolute wild man. You have one job to do, which is help us win games."

I said, "All right."

He said, "We're going to hit you ninth, so just go play."

I said, "Okay."

"And thanks for getting in shape."

"It's okay," I said. "I'm an ass kicker." And I walked out. He was laughing, because that's how I was.

But still, my personality hadn't really come out yet.

I really didn't have a close friend on the team. Kevin Youkilis had been in Triple A for a while with me, but he was a few years older. I hadn't really bonded with him the way I had bonded with David Murphy and Brandon Moss and Jon Lester.

And besides, Lester was a pitcher. Position players really don't hang out with pitchers.

Opening Day was in Kansas City, and while we lost, I went 2 for 3. By the tenth game, at home against Anaheim, however, I went 0 for 2 to drop to .222.

In the fifteenth game of the season, we lost to the Yankees 7-6 at Fenway. I went 0 for 2 and was lifted for a pinch hitter. My batting average was down to .158.

Man, it was a grind. They had put my locker next to Mike Lowell and Alex Cora. And Cora, he hadn't really opened up to me yet. He liked me as a guy, and I was very respectful of the veterans. If a veteran tells me to do something, then I'm going to drop everything and do it for them. I wasn't being an asshole—I was showing everybody respect. I could see the veterans liked me, but I stunk! I was hitting f—— .158! And I wasn't going to help them win by hitting .158 and being a nice guy.

It was tough. I kept telling myself, "These guys don't know yet. They've never seen the real me. When it comes out, it's going to be awesome."

I was getting hits here and there, and my average was still down at .182 in the beginning of May. I'd improved a little, but that wasn't saying much.

It was tough enough to break into this organization as a rookie and get used to everything, because when you come to Boston, everything feels like it's happening at 150 miles an hour. The fans, the media, everybody is thinking they know everything. People care about the Red Sox, they follow the Red Sox, they talk about the Red Sox. I knew even before I came up that Boston wasn't like a lot of cities. But I also don't think people understand that it can be tough on young players. Still, you have to fight through it, and once you get used to it you're fine.

In the end, that's why I always joke around with the media. I've got my list and there are people who I have to prove wrong. And when I prove them wrong, they're worried their time is coming. I think everyone knows I'll treat some media members a little bit differently than others.

A couple of things really showed me how it works in Boston when things get tough.

I was getting a lot of criticism from Jerry Remy, the Red Sox television color commentator. (Don Orsillo does the play-by-play.) The Rem Dawg played second base in his days with the Red Sox in the seventies and eighties, and the fans love the guy. I love him now, too, but it didn't really start off too well. The Rem Dawg was crushing me at the beginning. Really crushing me. Deservedly so, I guess, because when you don't play well you should be criticized. But at the time, I felt that the criticism was excessive. He'd try to be funny about it, but I didn't find it all that entertaining. There were times when he questioned whether I could make it in the big leagues, and wondered if I should be sent back down. The Rem Dawg said I was swinging too hard, and that I was overmatched by big-league pitching. He'd been a second baseman who hit seven career home runs and only two in his seven years with the Red Sox. Like Johnny Pesky, he was a left-handed hitter, and his style of play was all about getting on base.

ONCE I GOT going and was playing well, the Rem Dawg came around. That's when he started to seem a lot funnier to me. After that first month, we got along fine. When he was in the clubhouse before the game, writing the lineup down, we'd talk. Later that season, the fans elected him "President of Red Sox Nation," so when he came in, Alex Cora and I would say, "El Presidente!"

These days, I'll try to listen to him once in a while. My parents listen and they enjoy him. He has knowledge of the game and he's a great guy. But when you're not impressing the Rem Dawg, the fans aren't going to give you much of a break.

Another lesson in Boston Red Sox life took place just before the season. A reporter for one of the Boston papers said the problem was not just that I swung too hard, which people sometimes say, but also that I had a bad swing. This reporter decided my swing was "too long."

The reporter buried me in this article, saying that because my swing was too long, I'd never be a consistent major-league player. I didn't have any power. I wasn't strong enough. There was a big loop in my swing. At that point, entering the 2007 season, I only had eighty-nine at-bats in the big leagues. But I did have about a thousand minor-league at-bats, and I was a career .308 hitter in the minor leagues. But as I struggled a bit in the beginning, all of a sudden I was hearing about how the problem was my swing.

In my mind, I'd just started the season a little bit slow. Obviously that was in the back of my mind and frustrating me. Up through high school no one had ever said anything. I always hit at every level I played. In college, Coach Murphy never said one word to me.

Murph had always said, "Listen, just go play the game."

Dave Magadan, the Red Sox hitting coach, said, "Hey, listen. You're going to hit everywhere you're going to be. Just stay inside the ball like you always are and hit."

If I've hit everywhere from Little League to the major leagues and no one has tried to change my swing, how in the world is it possible that a reporter can crush a swing after only eighty-nine at-bats? But now there seemed to be a lot of talk about the problems with my swing.

I just thought, You know what, when I turn this around there are people who are going to look stupid! They shouldn't be writing things when they don't know what they're talking about. I understood that negativity sells, and so an article about my swing and how bad it is would obviously be read more than an article about a guy doing good things. I understood that gig. But it's another thing to write an article that's just not true.

My swing is actually really short to the ball. I'm just very violent in the box. I've got a big stride. I get down and swing hard. My swing is short. There's nothing long about it. That definitely set me off and frustrated me. It got in my mind a little bit. I'll be honest, I wasn't used to the media and the criticism like that. It's made me a stronger player, though.

I was coming home every night with all this adversity hitting me. It was tough on me, and it was really tough on my wife. Here we were, just married a few months, and when we were walking around town, people would be coming up to me and getting up in my face and saying, "Dude, you just *suck*!" I came home one night after a game, and Kelli was on the phone crying, telling her mother about all the things people were saying about me. I would take a cab ride, and the driver always seemed to have the sports-talk show on, and on the radio they always seemed to be crushing me. Everybody was saying they needed to send me back down to Pawtucket for more seasoning.

The way the fans were took Kelli by surprise. You'd turn on the television and the Red Sox were all that was being talked about and it was a little overwhelming for her. We learned quickly that we just had to try to stay away from it. You couldn't read the paper, couldn't watch the local news. There were boundaries to what we could do, and in that sense it sucked, but we had to get used to it. We were in a big market and that was what made your team good, the fan base and all the media coverage. We just had to deal with it as best we could.

After that first month of my rookie year, Kelli didn't like going to the games. Even now, she'll go in the playoffs, but for the most part when she comes to the park she'll sit in the wives' lounge and watch it on TV and listen to the Rem Dawg. More often, though, she stays home when I play. She doesn't have to be out seeing me play; she just cares about me as a person. Yes, she wants the Red Sox to do well, but her first priority is just to be a normal person and stay down-to-earth. That's why it was difficult for her when the fans were being hard on me in those first weeks of the season.

People were giving me all this shit, and I was just nodding and saying, "I know, yeah, you're right. I do suck right now." I wasn't candy-coating it. I knew it. Nobody really needed to tell me I sucked. At one point I spoke to Coach Murphy from Arizona State. He told me what Harvey Dorfman had told me five years earlier: don't be a wimp, just get out there and do it. He said to me, "Pedro, you're five foot seven, you're balding, and you're not even an athlete . . . How the hell are you even in the big leagues? Figure that out and then go get it done."

It was great to have him lighten it up for me. Later that night, I texted back to him. I wanted to make Murph know he had helped.

I wrote, *Look out, I'm about to put Red Sox Nation on my back!*

You have to stay positive, because it's a long season and things eventually find their level. At that lowest point, I'd only played in fifteen games and had just forty at-bats. Over the course of 450 or 500 at-bats or whatever it may end up being, you'll see what you have. I knew that I would get my bleeders and my seeing-eye ground balls. Those hits were going to come, right along with the hard-hit line-outs that seemed to be happening way too much at that point. Obviously, if three or four or five more of those line drives had fallen in for hits, then I would have been hitting .280 and everybody would have said, "He's off to a great start." But it was situations like this that people didn't understand. In Kansas City, the opening series of the season, I hit three line drives that got caught. If those had fallen in, everybody would have acted like I was the greatest hitter of all time.

Alex Cora

Infielder, New York Mets

Boston Red Sox Infielder, 2006–2008

Going into spring training in 2007, everybody was talking about how it was going to be a competition between myself and Dustin for the starting second-base position. But going in, I felt like I knew my role with the Red Sox. I knew why they had given me a two-year contract at the beginning of 2006, after I'd been traded to the Red Sox from the Cleveland Indians in the middle of the 2005 season. I wasn't naïve. It's the way the Red Sox do things to build their team. They trust their minor-league system to identify and develop talented players. At least that's how they've done it in the last few years.

For the 2007 season, they were looking for a guy who could spell Dustin early in the season, until he got his feet wet playing in the major leagues. If he were to fail, they wanted someone who could be trusted to handle the position. I was that guy, and I knew my role.

I can be very honest and say I would have loved to have played every day. At the same time, I knew where I fit in with the team and its goals, and that was a far more important thing. It wasn't like I was going to be mad—if I were someone else, I might have been mad, especially early in the season, the way he was struggling and the way I was swinging the bat. I was hitting well, but all of a sudden I wasn't getting at-bats.

But I knew that for the Boston Red Sox to be a championship team, we needed Dustin Pedroia to play second base and we needed me to be a utility guy, ready to go when I was needed.

Getting to know Dustin was a step-by-step thing. When he was called up at the end of 2006, I hadn't really gotten to know him. We had only played a month together. And I knew how it was when you're called up to the big leagues late in the season: you're so into what you want to prove and what you want to do, there's really no chance to get to know people.

We got to know each other a lot better in spring training of 2007. Yeah, we talked about playing second base and all that, and we talked about a lot of other things.

Little by little we began getting comfortable with each other. It's like any other relationship. The thing that I came to really like and respect about Dustin, and the thing that made me feel he's a really great person, was that even though he was scuffling and struggling, he wasn't like a lot of the kids who get called up now, who don't want to listen to anybody. He showed respect for people, wanted to learn, and wanted to be a good teammate.

We'd talk about baseball—not our situation, but something general about baseball—and we'd start getting that trust in each other. To tell you the truth, I began to see him as the little brother I never had, because I was the youngest in my family. I started trying to talk to him a little, and pushing him a little, and getting him going. I don't want to say that's exactly what Theo and Tito brought me in to do, but it was part of why I was there. It was like, "Help him out, help him out."

Knowing my role, and knowing what I am expected to do for the team, is probably why I still have a job in the big leagues. I've been playing for a long time, and obviously my goal is to play every day. But you need to know and understand what you are. Everybody wants to play every day, and if they tell you something else, they're lying. At the same time, you don't want to be trying to keep someone down, because when October comes, you might be going home early. For things to happen the way you want them to, you have to have every piece click in together. Dustin was a piece of the team, although at the beginning we didn't know if he would turn out to be the starting second baseman.

It helped a lot that he was right next to me in the locker room. It's like it is with your next-door neighbor. You start talking to him, then you start feeling what he's feeling about certain things, then you try to help him out when he's got something he needs.

I've been in the big leagues a while, but I was a rookie once, too. And I had really struggled. My first year in the big leagues, with the Los Angeles Dodgers in 2000, I hit .238 and my second year I hit .217. So I know what that feels like. I was playing in a place where we were expected to win. To tell the truth, there were some guys there who tried to help me a little, but I don't know if I ever felt comfortable there in those first few years. Now, as a veteran guy, I don't want to make a younger guy feel that way. The way I was feeling, when I came up to the major leagues, I didn't want anyone having to go through feeling that way. I didn't have to go too far out of the way—I was still working on my craft and working on my game—but our friendship just clicked.

12

Turning a Corner

A few times early in the 2007 season, Tito gave me days off, which wasn't a good thing—I was being given days off because I sucked. And meanwhile Alex Cora was hitting something like .400—he was just raking.

We lost one of those games, and I was pissed, both because we lost and because I wasn't playing. After the game, Cora was sitting there, and he put his hand on my shoulder and said, "Listen, kid, you're going to be all right. I know it."

I looked at him. "You think?"

He said, "Yeah, I do."

It was great to have a guy like Cora, who was always about the team, say that. Here was a guy who played the same position as me and could have found it easy to keep a distance. But instead, he was the guy who had my back.

Even Manny came up to me, because by now he had finally figured out who I was, and said, "Hey, Pedey. You need to calm down."

"Okay, Manny."

I was in the batting cage, trying really hard to work things out. Meanwhile, Manny, on the field, was always joking around. He's something to see. He's got bubble gum all over the place and his hair is flying everywhere. When we were in the batting cage, he'd have these conversations with me, or he'd make jokes. His conversations were short, to the point, and usually funny. Then he'd just walk away. That was Manny.

He said to me, "If you hit .300 and win Rookie of the Year, I'm going to buy you a Rolex."

It meant a lot to me for him to say something encouraging. I said, "Thanks, Manny, but .300 is a long-ass way away and so is Rookie of the Year." He just walked away, smiling.

I appreciated the gesture, and that he now knew who I was and had some encouragement for me. But I have to admit that I was thinking to myself, Yeah, you're crazy, buddy.

ON MAY 4, a month into the season, we went out to Minnesota, away from Fenway and away from some of that atmosphere I was dealing with. In the second game of the series, we were facing Johan Santana, a lefty, so Cora wasn't going to play. Alex had gone 3 for 3 in the first game of the series, to take his average to .406. I thought, Okay, I better start f—— doing something.

I'd been working hard at trying to slow my game down. It's funny, but when I was playing in those big stadiums, it felt like I was faster than the game. I couldn't get myself slowed down to a pace that felt right.

Playing under that dome slowed the game down for me.

So when Johan threw his fastball at about ninety-five miles an hour, it felt like it was coming at eighty-five. We lost the game 2-1, but I ended up going 2 for 2, with a double and a walk. I was on base three times and had a good game, which upped my average from .182 to .206. I'd had only sixty at-bats so far. That's what I kept telling myself: "Only sixty at-bats; you'll be fine."

The next afternoon, we faced Sidney Ponson. I went 3 for 4, and two of the hits were doubles. I thought, Damn, I've hit three doubles in two days. I'm starting to come on. Now I was hitting .239.

I could see the light now. Next we went to Toronto. I hit my first home run in the second inning with two outs and two on, to put us up 3-1 early in the game. That series, I went 4 for 8 and was now up to .267.

We got back to Boston and I was feeling like things were still turning. On that Friday night against Baltimore, I went 0 for 3 to drop to .254, but what I was hearing was, *This guy's got power, this guy can hit.*

I did an interview with a local cable television guy in Boston. And he just blasted me.

My attitude is, if you ask me a question, I'm going to answer it—I'm respectful of the job the media have to do. If I'm playing bad, come at me—it's nobody's fault but my own. But I felt that all through this, some people were just kicking me when I was down.

I was doing this interview on camera, where I couldn't see the guy—it was one of those interviews where he's at the studio. But I have him in my ear, and it's live. And he kept saying *slump, slump, slump*, using that word.

I said, "You know, it's only a little more than sixty at-bats. I'm trying to break it down and turn it into a positive, and I'm coming out of that, and growing up as a player, and you guys are watching that right in front of your eyes."

He said, "But Dustin, you're in a fishbowl."

And I'm thinking, Fishbowl. Yeah, I got your f—— fishbowl right here.

From then on, I made it perfectly clear that whoever was going to crush me was going to get crushed, too. And I turned all that shit people were throwing at me into motivation. I was going to prove everybody wrong. And if they didn't like me, then f— them. I am who I am: I'm five foot seven, and I'm 170 pounds, and what else am I going to do but lay out rockets and help win games? And other than that, take care of my wife? That was basically it. Those two jobs were what I needed to do.

The Red Sox veterans helped me a ton. They all knew that I had to be a part of this so we could win. If I could get on base in the ninth spot, then we could do some damage, because if Julio Lugo was driving in runs batting lead-off, then it was going to make David, Manny, and J. D. Drew's job a lot easier.

I think a lot of people overlooked that, saying that just because I was in the ninth spot I didn't really have to hit, I just needed to play defense. Well, that might be true in some ways, but if I could produce, say, in a Yankees series, then that would be huge. My job was to help us win games. I wasn't going to drive in a hundred runs— at least, I wasn't looking like I was going to do that kind of thing right then—but my job was to do the most I possibly could to help us win, and to get used to playing in the big leagues.

On a team, every guy on the roster is part of it. It takes the entire team to win a championship. It meant a lot to me that the guys were showing confidence in me. Even if I was struggling, I was going to do everything I could to pull through it, and because of that I knew they had my back.

From then on, I was getting more confident in myself. I started coming out of it.

On May 22, when we beat the Yankees in New York, I was batting .260.

MY FIRST SERIES at Yankee Stadium, back in April, had been pretty exciting for me. We'd won two out of the three games. I'd played in two of them, and I'd gone 1 for 6, still hitting at .182.

Now, nearly a month later, I was seeing my hitting coming together, and I was feeling more confident. In late May, we went back into Yankee Stadium for a three-game series, with the Yankees in fourth place and about ten games back. They were hoping to gain ground with a sweep. It would also be my first taste of Red Sox–Yankees controversy in a rivalry that has had a lot of that.

I sat out the first game. Alex Cora played second base and got a hit to keep his average at .333, but the Yankees beat us, 6-2. In the second game, that Tuesday night, we had Julian Tavarez pitching against Mike Mussina.

In the top of the first, Manny hit a bomb, scoring Youkilis and Ortiz to put us up 3-0. In the seventh inning, with us up 4-2, we got three more to take a 7-2 lead. Then, with one out in the bottom of the eighth, Derek Jeter singled and Hideki Matsui walked. Alex Rodriguez walked to load the bases.

The next batter, Jorge Posada, hit a ground ball to Mike Lowell, who got it right to me for a potential double play. As I stepped on the base, Rodriguez came at me with his left elbow up into my belt.

He got a shot in, and Posada beat my throw to first. Jeter scored to make it 7-3, which would be the final.

I didn't say anything to Rodriguez after he hit me. But after the game I said to the media that the next time he came in at me, he'd better come in low or he might get the ball in his face.

It wasn't a threat, just the reality of the way the game is played. In the second inning of that same game, I'd tried to break up a double play sliding into Jeter. But I'd come in low, the way it's done.

I wasn't all that worried about A-Rod's slide. It was just something that happened. That was the end of that.

On one hand, there are always those unwritten rules of the game. You don't come at the second baseman's knees. You don't step on the first baseman's foot while he's stretching. Yeah, you play the game to win but you don't do certain things. Everybody plays the game hard. Everybody plays the game to win and they play clean.

But there are certain situations where some guys want it a little too much and they get out of line, or they do something they don't necessarily want to do—it just happens. The game is fast. This game is not in television-style slow motion, and so some players can get out of control.

I definitely do it, too. There are times I'm a little out of control on the base paths. It's not that I'm trying to do something chippy, and other players know that. I'm definitely not going to take a cheap shot at anybody.

There are other rules, too.

Obviously you protect your teammates. If a pitcher is throwing at our guys, then our pitcher will throw at his guys. So the players usually patrol each side. That's why baseball is so special: the unwritten rules and traditions about the way it is played. Each team is out trying to win a game and all your teammates are on your side and you're working together to win.

A week later, after a May 29 game when we beat Cleveland 4-2 at Fenway Park, I was batting .302. It was the first time I'd gone over .300 in the big leagues. The Red Sox had a 36-15 record, a five-game winning streak, and were in first place. We'd been in first place since April 14.

The next big turning point was against the Giants, in Boston in the middle of June. Tito moved me to batting second in the lineup.

On June 15, I got to play against the team I'd always considered my favorite, against the player who was always the one I thought was the best. That Friday night, the San Francisco Giants came to Fenway Park. It was the first time the Giants had ever played a regular-season game at Fenway in their history, and the first time they'd played the Red Sox at Fenway since the 1912 World Series, so it felt extraordinary. And my childhood hero, Barry Bonds, was right across the field in the dugout. He was at 747 home runs, chasing Hank Aaron, but he'd been stuck there for a while.

Before the game, I thought I might try to say hello to him, but there was no way that was going to happen. With so many members of the media around Bonds before the game, I couldn't just walk up and talk to him. The media that were following his home-run record chase was like an army, with Barry in the middle of them, just doing his thing.

When he came up to bat in the first inning, the Giants were leading 1-0, with Mark Sweeney on third base after a double and a groundout. Bonds stepped into the box and everybody at Fenway was on their feet and booing. People in the stands were waving signs with asterisks on them.

In that first at-bat, he launched the second pitch he got from Julian Tavarez. It went right up the right-field line. It was so high it went over the top of the Pesky Pole, as the right-field pole is known to the Fenway Faithful. The crowd went totally quiet, watching that ball go. From where I was it was hard to tell, but the first-base umpire waved it off. Foul ball. Bonds thought it was fair. You could tell he was a little pissed, because he stood there giving the umpire the Look, but he was smiling when he went back to the batter's box. The Giants' manager, Bruce Bochy, came out and argued it, but then Barry got back in the box. He took the next pitch for a ball.

Then he ended that at-bat by popping up. To me. I moved out onto the grass, got my glove up, and waited. And there it was. Barry Bonds had popped out to me.

J. D. Drew was leading off that night. On the first pitch, the Giants' Barry Zito hit J. D.

I came up next. And put a line drive over the Monster. With that bomb, I was only 742 home runs behind Barry Bonds on the all-time list.

It was awesome; it just kept going. In the third inning I singled off Zito, and in the fourth I singled off him again to score J. D. and make the score 6-2. I singled again in the sixth. And in the eighth I doubled to score Coco Crisp and Julio Lugo, then I scored on a Wily Mo Pena ground ball to put us up 10-2.

In my first game against the team I'd grown up rooting for as a kid, I'd gone 5 for 5, with five runs batted in. I don't think I'd had a five-hit, five-runs-batted-in game since I was in Little League. I had a little bit more intensity, I think, because I was kind of pissed at the Giants. I hold a bit of a grudge against a few teams that could have drafted me, especially in that 2001 draft where no one had even taken a chance on me as their fiftieth-round pick. You always play hard, but you want to make sure you show them, "Hey, you had your chance."

And the San Francisco Giants was the team I loved, and was one of those teams that easily could have seen what I can do. I was in their backyard, but they didn't want to take a chance on me. The Arizona Diamondbacks were the same way. When I was playing in college they had a chance to see me for about ninety home games over my three years. I was only five miles away. It's one of those things where they probably just didn't think I could do it. In the 2004 draft they had the fifty-sixth overall pick and passed on me, picking outfielder Jonathan Zeringue of Louisiana State.

I'm pretty sure that both those teams, and maybe a few others, regret their lack of interest in me as a draft pick.

MY AVERAGE AFTER that 5-for-5 game against the Giants went up to .331. The Red Sox were eight and a half games up in first place.

In the third game of that series, on Sunday afternoon, I got to talk to Barry Bonds. He got on second base and I looked over at him. He said, "Hey, little man, you went to ASU?"

"Yeah."

I talked to him for a little bit about ASU. It was definitely cool to play against a guy I had watched as a young kid. Later in that game, Bonds got his home run at Fenway, off Tim Wakefield, who had been his teammate with the Pirates back in the 1990s. But we swept the series and moved on to play at Atlanta and San Diego to finish interleague play.

It was getting to the point that everybody knew we were the best team in baseball, and I was part of it. I wasn't just the number-nine hitter now. I felt like I was an important part of the lineup. I wasn't just a guy about whom people would say, "Yeah, he plays good defense." Sure I'd made some plays—against the Yankees I'd made a diving play on a ball going up the middle. But none of that gets noticed if you're not hitting the ball. The little things don't count unless everything's going great.

When I think about the 2007 season, that's one of the things I'm proudest of: even when I wasn't hitting, I was finding ways to help us win, whatever way I could. That's what my job was. That's what I'd been told to do. The best part of that 2007 season, regardless of the other things that would happen, was how when I was hitting down around .150, I'd take the field every day and do absolutely anything I could to help us win even when I wasn't hitting the ball, or when the balls I was hitting were right at people. That was special to me.

WHEN YOU'RE A rookie in the major leagues, everything is a new experience. In late August we played the Yankees at Yankee Stadium, with Roger Clemens pitching. We hadn't faced him before because he'd only joined the Yankees in mid-June. We'd played the Yankees twelve times before that. Now I was facing a guy who seemed a certain Hall of Famer.

It's exciting facing all-time great players. I'm a fan of the game as well, and when you're facing a Roger Clemens, or you get a chance to play a Barry Bonds, you're playing against guys who have been around for so long and have been so great for so long, you catch yourself sitting back and admiring what these guys can do.

I remember watching A-Rod hit a particular home run. This ball was *launched*. I remember watching the ball in the air, thinking, Holy shit! That's an absolute bomb from one of the best players of all time.

It's special being on the same field playing against a guy like that, and trying to beat him and his team. I'll have a chance to reflect more on that when my career is all done, but when it's happening, my face is in the dirt and I'm trying to help our team win. And the only way to beat a guy like that is to do the little things to overcome not being as talented as he is.

The first time I got in the box with Roger Clemens on the mound, I had to stay focused on what I had to do.

He hit me with a pitch.

IN THE MIDDLE of the 2007 season, with all that was happening on the field, there was a moment when both my wife and I were reminded of more important things.

Kelli found another mole on her neck that didn't seem right. There had been the tumor in her thigh, before I met her, and then two years later another mole that had to be removed, and now this one. She went to the doctor to have it checked and the doctor said it had to be cut out. It was precautionary, but it always makes you worry a little bit.

It's always a nervous time when something like that happens. Kelli had told me that when she had her first diagnosis, even though the mole itself was really small, the tumor underneath turned out to be big. But she also knew that she hadn't been as careful as she should. Before our wedding the previous November, she'd even gone to a tanning booth.

In late June, we were on a road trip out to San Diego and Seattle. While we were in Seattle, Dawn Timlin, the wife of relief pitcher Mike Timlin, invited Kelli to climb Mount Rainier with her. Dawn is really athletic, and Kelli agreed to go. Kelli covered herself in sunscreen, but up at that altitude the sun is intense, and reflects off the snow. Kelli ended up with a second-degree sunburn, despite all her precautions. Not long after, this mole appeared on her neck, and it looked a little shaky.

It was upsetting to Kelli because she thought she had done everything she needed to do to be safe. But we both realized that it's just something she has to be more careful about than ever before.

When she had the mole removed, it wasn't as bad as the first occurrence, but she was still upset. Her biggest fear was that everyone was going to see a terrible scar.

I told her, "Kelli, chill out. It's not going to be that big and who cares that it's on your neck? The only one who should care is me, and guess what? I don't. You're going to be all right. I'm always going to love you the same. It's not like you're going to be ugly, because you're beautiful in every way."

She has to see those scars every day and it upsets her. But she's doing everything she can to help people out, and that's one of the things that makes her a special person.

Kelli got involved in efforts to educate young girls that melanoma isn't something you mess around with.

We were both asked by Major League Baseball to participate in an awareness campaign called "Play Smart When It Comes to the

Sun." Not only does the program screen major-league players and team staff members for skin cancer risk, it also has awareness programs that reach out to the community.

I said to Kelli, "You need to stand behind your word on this."

From then on, both of us were more aware. She swore off tanning beds and she made sure to use sunscreen, stay in the shade, and protect her skin. As for me, I was more aware about using sunscreen when we were playing day games.

Kelli's willingness to work hard to get the word out has been awesome. And I know she's had a positive effect. When I was at an appearance in 2008, a girl of high school age came up to me and said, "Your wife changed my life about tanning and tanning beds."

She took me by surprise, so I ended up talking to her a little bit. She told me, "I don't do that stuff anymore and I wear sunscreen. I was addicted to the sun just like she was." For Kelli even to impact just that one young girl's life, well, that's good enough already. And I'm sure there are many more girls she's helped. Kelli had had no idea how bad tanning beds can be—twenty minutes in one is like baking in the natural sun for three hours without any sunscreen. More women are getting melanoma at young ages, as Kelli did, and some people think it may be because of the number of teenage girls who are going to tanning places all the time.

We were fortunate: Kelli was fine. A lot of great things happened in 2007, with Kelli's recovery and her work to raise awareness definitely among the most important.

I FINISHED THE 2007 season strong.

After hitting .182 in April, I hit .415 in May. The team had moved into first place in the twelfth game of the year, and for the next 150 games we stayed at the top of the division. May was as good for me as April had been bad. From there, I felt strong, never dropping below .300.

One reason is that as the year went on, my personality began to come out.

The other guys always poked fun at me, but at first I wouldn't say anything; I'd just laugh back. They probably thought I was a good kid, because I'd just get crushed by them and wouldn't say anything. As the year went on, though, I started firing back. I wasn't taking shit from anybody, and they liked that. Mike Lowell and I became best friends; Alex Cora and I became best friends. You could tell a family was starting. Winning obviously helped that, but it was more than that. Here I'd been, hitting a buck and a half, and the veteran utility infielder who's sitting at the locker right next to me had been rooting for me, wanting me to do better. You don't see that anywhere else.

I had Tim Wakefield helping me out. He'd been in the big leagues for fifteen years. Curt Schilling was helping me out, too. They just encouraged me and treated me like a teammate. None of these guys had to do that. But I'd been fighting my ass off and they knew it.

BY THAT SUMMER, I felt like I was seeing major-league pitching well.

Your eyes get used to it. Everybody in the majors has good eyes. Even the guys who say they don't, their eyes work very well. Everybody adjusts to how fast the game is. You have to: You're up there facing a 98- or 99-mile-per-hour fastball. A normal person stepping into the box would say, "Holy shit! I didn't even see that!"

As a major-league player, you see it and you know it's coming in fast, and you can pick up the ball. That's just a gift God gave us. It's a part of who we are. Just like pitchers. How many guys can throw over ninety-plus miles per hour? Not that many: mostly guys pitching in the major leagues. You can't grab some guy off the street and say, "Okay, here's the ball. Try to get David Ortiz out."

Some gifts are just God-given. If God makes your arm a lightning bolt, or gives you great vision, that's just who you are.

I have something like 20/10 eyesight. All I know is that my eyesight is perfect. To be honest with you, I don't read very well, even though I can see the words. My eyes are just made differently. They're made to see fastballs coming in, but not to read a book.

THAT YEAR I got to see what makes Terry Francona such a great manager.

Tito is a baseball thinker. Tito manages smart.

First of all, he understands it's a 162-game season. If we have a long road trip or something like eight or nine games in a row, Tito isn't going to blow the bullpen out the first day. He's not going to do anything to ruin what we're trying to do in the long run. He isn't going to blow out our starting pitching early in the year. He is intelligent about having a plan for the whole season, to make our team strong at the end. Sometimes in the regular season, you have to manage for tomorrow.

In my first full season, I learned about that from watching Tito: how to take a team through a full 162 games and be a better team at the end than when the season began. I haven't seen anyone do it better than him—obviously I haven't played for another team or another manager, but you can see what he does with our team.

He has a plan, and the coaching staff has bought into it. They're a major reason why the team has been up near a hundred wins in all but one of the seasons he has managed the Red Sox. Yes, it's the players doing their jobs, but the coaching staff makes it easier for us to go out there and have success. Tito has surrounded us with a great group of coaches, and they all work to help us get to the postseason.

When the postseason does come, he manages to win the game we're playing in. In the postseason, you don't manage for tomorrow: it's all right then.

Before the game begins, I know where I'm going to be positioned defensively because of the coaching and scouting staff. As players, we live and die by those scouting reports. When you talk about the team, it extends past the guys who are on the roster. For defense, we have meetings before the game two minutes after the lineups are posted for the opposing team. Luis Alicea, our first-base coach at the time, would go through the other team's lineup and tell us where to play each batter. Now that I'm used to a lot of the hitters, and have watched a lot of tape of the other teams, I try to position myself a bit more by feel, but that's coming off the scouting.

Dave Magadan, our hitting coach, has worked a lot with all of us. He's worked with me so much he's probably sick of me. I've never seen another hitting coach do the job the way he does.

Mags gets to the clubhouse early, and when the players get in there's a sheet on each player's chair. It will be a breakdown on the starting pitcher—what he features, velocity he's had of late, what he did in his last start, and percentages of what pitches he throws in certain counts. It's unbelievably detailed. There's not a thing that's not on that sheet—how he holds runners on base, how he pitches with the bases loaded, etc.

We also have sheets on each relief pitcher, but when a guy comes in from the bullpen during a game, I'll usually go over to Mags and ask him to refresh my memory on that pitcher's tendencies. There are so many damn pitchers—I'm not that much of a machine, but Mags is when it comes to knowing the opposition.

When a pitcher is running in from the bullpen, Mags will be saying, "He pitches ninety-two to ninety-five, hard slider, changeup, and the split is his out pitch." Or "ninety-five to ninety-seven, likes to elevate, gets outs with his fastball up." Mags is great because he's always one step ahead—if a guy is warming up in the bullpen, Mags already has his stuff out and is going over it.

During a game, the other side of the infield will communicate about positioning—Mike Lowell will talk with shortstops Jed Lowrie or Julio Lugo. On my side of the infield, Youk and I will make sure we're on the same page. I'll be saying, "Youk, you can get the line more, and I'll be over in the hole," or "Youk, I'm playing deeper, you can give more room." Or "Youk, I'm in the middle, you need to come up with me." He'll do the same. Youk and I will communicate the whole game, pretty much on every pitch. That's why Youk and I play so well together. We want to get to the damn ball and get an out. It's really simple, but by moving a step or two one way or another, and getting to that one extra ball to get that one extra out, we can win the game with defense. In 162 games it might just win us one game—and we might win the division by one game. And home-field advantage could hinge on that one game we won on that one out on that one ground ball. That's how important those little things are in baseball.

ON THE NIGHT of September 1, 2007, we played the Orioles at Fenway, with Clay Buchholz pitching his second career start for us. Clay had been called up to pitch in Anaheim a couple of weeks before, then was called back up from Pawtucket for this one start. He was going to be sent down after the game, no matter how he did. Clay was young and was being brought along. That afternoon, Tito had said to the media, "I don't care if he pitches a no-hitter tonight. He's going back to Pawtucket after the game."

Clay went ahead and did that. We got an 8-0 lead by the end of the sixth, and he still hadn't given up a hit, so most of the focus was on whether he'd be the first Red Sox rookie ever to pitch a no-hit game.

I'd been part of no-hitters when I was younger; in fact, in high school our team was involved in winning three no-hitters in a row in the 1999 season; we then lost one.

But this wasn't high school. This was a major-league no-hitter he had going. Everybody could feel the excitement growing over the course of the game.

In the top of the seventh with no outs, I made a play that helped save the no-hitter.

I'll never forget that play, for a lot of reasons. One was that when I was coming out for the top of the inning, I'd put a humongous load of sunflower seeds in my mouth, and now I was standing out at my position thinking, F—, I just put an entire bag of sunflower seeds in my mouth. It was a little hard to breathe. And besides that, I had to pee.

So really, I was hoping it would be a quick inning. Miguel Tejada was up, and I was thinking, Whatever happens here, if the ball comes my way I just hope I don't either choke on my sunflower seeds or pee my pants. That was pretty much the only thing on my mind the whole inning.

Sure enough, Tejada hit a chopper, bounding over Clay and heading right up the middle. I went after it, and I swear if you look closely at the replay, you can see the sunflower seeds just spraying out of my mouth. I mean, they were just flying everywhere.

I knocked the ball down and got the throw over just in time to beat Tejada, who tried a headfirst slide into the base. That would be the closest the Orioles came to breaking it up. Clay finished the game by striking out Nick Markakis, and everybody mobbed Clay. People were also patting me on the back for getting to that ball in the seventh.

I think all those seeds shooting out of my mouth actually gave me the speed to get to that ball. In fact I'm sure of that.

Dave Magadan

Hitting Coach

Boston Red Sox

The first time I got a look at Dustin Pedroia was when I got the job as hitting coach with the Red Sox and got video of all the guys. It was interesting because all the video I had of Dustin had been shot from the side, with none looking in from center field. But what I saw from the video was that while he was very unorthodox in the way he swung from the waist down, from the waist up he's very direct to the ball.

He's short—not short short, but he's short to the ball. And he seemed to barrel up a lot of balls. No matter if the pitch was up, down, away, or reaching for it, he always seemed to get the bat head on the ball.

When I finally got to see some video shot from center field when he was called up in the later part of the 2006 season, I was seeing how much he bailed, stepping away from the plate with his front foot. His stride was going toward the shortstop, not straight ahead, but he was still managing to have pretty good plate coverage, especially for a guy with short arms.

When Tito asked me to look at it and break it down, my main concern was why he had struggled after he was called up from Pawtucket in 2006. I worried that opposing pitchers were going to start pounding him off the plate. I was concerned that they were going to start throwing him breaking balls away, and that Dustin wouldn't be able to cover both sides of the plate. With the way he bailed, I worried that he was not going to be able to cover the outside of the plate.

It remained a concern for me throughout spring training in 2007. Dustin took his swing into the year and struggled in the first month of the season. We continued to have some worries because of that, but the one thing that was never wavering was his confidence in himself. He seemed to always know it was just a matter of time before he was going to start hitting. When someone feels that way, and it's genuine—and there was nothing fake about it with Pedey—you just stick with him. Thank God we did.

As far as his swing is concerned, he's unorthodox from the waist down because he's got a lot going on. But from the waist up, he's short to the ball and he stays inside the ball. I call it "bat lag." The barrel of his bat kind of lags behind and that gives him just enough time to read the pitch, even when he's fooled. You see him do that a lot. He's bailing and his shoulder is going up, but he still has that bat head dragging where he can give himself a chance to hit the ball the other way. It's fun to watch him get to some of those pitches.

As a coach, you start thinking, Well, can we get him to start striding more toward the pitcher? Will that help? I wasn't really concerned as much with his upper half, other than when he was striding toward the shortstop and pulling his shoulder off the ball.

He was striding toward short but his body was staying on the baseball.

The one and only thing I talked to him about when he was struggling was his shoulders: keeping them more parallel to the ground. It was all connected to his head. When his head tilts, like anybody else, his shoulders tilt. He was getting underneath a lot of balls, especially pitches that were up in the zone. Instead of getting on top of them, he was getting underneath balls and hitting a lot of lazy fly balls to right.

Really, the only thing we worked on was keeping his head a little more upright rather than getting it tilted in his stride. He was able to do it and make the adjustment by just doing stuff off the tee. It had an immediate result.

What was a little surprising was for him to hit the amount of home runs he hit in his second season. He went from eight in 2007 to seventeen in 2008. We really didn't see that coming this soon. But he's such a quick study and he knows how he's going to get pitched to and he starts looking for pitches in locations. When he gets his pitch and he's looking for it, and it's in a spot where he wants it, he's going to square it up and hit it a long way.

But a lot of his success is about attitude. He uses what's written about him, especially the negative stuff, as something that can be to his advantage. It lights a fire under him. Not that he needs a fire lit under him, but it's really a huge motivating factor for him. I know a lot of stuff that was written about him when he was struggling, you know, about how he needed to get sent back down to Pawtucket, and about how Alex Cora should have been playing in his place. Pedey really used that as a motivational factor. He doesn't forget about it.

He talks a lot about it in the cage when he's doing his stuff. He kind of winds himself up. His pregame stuff, he's never in the cage saying, "Okay, let's get this over and done with." It's always with a purpose and it's always done in a way so he can begin his gear-up for the game.

I have never really been around a guy who is as high energy as he is in a positive way. The one guy who comes to mind is Luis Gonzalez, when I played with him in Houston in 1995. He was pretty similar. He was always smiling and always in a good mood. Pedey is the same way. He's always very positive. He's the type of guy who not only cares about the game, he cares about his teammates. He cares about everybody who is involved with the Red Sox.

13

Champions

Late in the 2007 season, my left hand really started hurting. The pain came on in early September. I couldn't figure out what was causing it. I'd been hit by a pitch on August 22 at Tampa Bay. It had happened in the third inning, with Edwin Jackson pitching, and it had hurt enough for me to leave the game. But I was back in the lineup two days later against the White Sox in Chicago. Still, by September it was hurting more, and it was also hard for me to hold the bat.

I finally went to Tito and told him. He thanked me for being straight with him and told me to get to a doctor.

An MRI showed there was a break in the hamate bone, a small bone near the heel of the hand. I don't know for sure if the injury was from that pitch in Tampa Bay or from something else. It may have happened swinging the bat. The injury is common for hitters and golfers because the end of the bat (or club) rests against that bone. I changed my grip on the bat, and that seemed to work somewhat.

I wasn't going to shut it down. There were too many games left to play, and I wasn't coming out if I could help it. The good news was that even though the hand hurt, the doctors told me that continuing to play wasn't going to cause any further injury to the bone or the nerves. I'd just have to deal with the pain. In the end, the physical pain was minor compared to the way the season had started out.

September was a rush for the finish line. On September 4, we were in first place by seven games. On September 9, we were in first place by a game and a half, the smallest lead we'd had since early in the season. We had lost two out of three to the Yankees at Fenway, then we'd gone to Toronto and lost three straight. That was only the second time all season we'd lost four straight games.

But we went on to win six of the next eight games. On September 29, we clinched the division after we beat the Minnesota Twins at home and the Orioles beat the Yankees 10-9 in the tenth inning the day before. Our game ended at a little after nine-thirty, and we sat and waited for the outcome of the Orioles and Yankees. That game ended just before 11 P.M., and a lot of the fans had stayed at the ballpark to watch it on a live feed on the Fenway scoreboard. It was the first time the Red Sox had won the American League East division in twelve years. The champagne got popped, and it felt good to be division champions. Some of us went back up to the field just to take in the moment. Tito lit a big cigar for himself. But we knew we hadn't reached the goal we'd set way back in spring training. There was more baseball to play.

After a loss to the Twins on the final day, we finished the 2007 season in first place, two games ahead of the Yankees. And after being at a point where I was having people on the street telling me I sucked, I finished the season with a .317 average.

•   •   •

WE WENT INTO the American League Division Series against the Angels. They finished in first place in the West, six games up on Oakland, and had won ninety-four games, two fewer than we did. It was going to be a battle.

Those divisional playoffs were weird, because you played a game, then had a day off, or two days off. That was strange for me. I'm a big rhythm guy—I have to play every day to be at my best. I look back and think maybe that was part of what screwed me up at the beginning of the season. I wasn't playing every day, and I couldn't get my timing down because I wasn't out there enough. But I wasn't going to say anything about that; I wasn't running the team.

I struggled in that divisional series against the Angels. I went 0 for 4 the first game at Fenway, which we won 4-0. The second game, which was also in Boston, I went 1 for 5 and we won 6-3. I doubled to start the fifth inning, moved to third on a grounder, then scored to tie the game when Mike Lowell hit a sacrifice fly to center. It had been 3-3 in the bottom of the ninth when Manny hit a walk-off home run with Julio Lugo and David Ortiz on base.

But the third game, out at Anaheim, I got an RBI double in the eighth with us up 2-0. That inning we broke it open, scoring seven runs to go up 9-0, and winning 9-1, clinching the series.

But I'd only gone 2 for 13, for a .154 average.

We saw the Indians had won, and their pitching was a shut-down staff. They had C. C. Sabathia, Fausto Carmona, Rafael Betancourt, and a lot of other good pitchers in the bullpen. Joe Borowski had forty-five saves during the season. And their hitters were good. Travis Hafner could hit home runs, and Kenny Lofton was forty but could get on and steal bases. We knew it would be a tough series.

After we beat them 10-3 in the first game at Fenway, I thought we were invincible. Then in Game Two, we went into the eleventh inning tied at 6-6, and they scored seven runs in the top of the inning and beat us 13-6. After the game, I thought, Shit, we're not invincible after all. I hadn't lost a postseason game before. We had just run through the Angels with no problem, and the Angels, well, Mike Scioscia had gotten those guys locked in.

We headed to Cleveland. The atmosphere was crazy. I mean, we were playing in a jail. That place was rocking, they were all waving their stupid towels, and now I was leading off the game with a broken hand.

It hadn't hurt enough to keep me from playing, but it hurt. After two games of the series, I was 2 for 8. I was thinking, This is adversity at its highest point. We had been through some shit, but now I'm in this, playing for my lifelong dream.

But we lost the next two games in Cleveland, 4-2 and then 7-3. I went 0 for 4 in Game Three and 1 for 4 in Game Four. I was 3 for 16 in the series at that point. And the hand injury was still bothering me. Cold weather was making it hurt more. And when Jake Westbrook struck me out in the first inning of Game Three, I tried checking my swing, and the pain was unbelievable. Things just weren't going well.

WE HAD A meeting after Game Four, and it helped. We knew that all the goals we wanted to accomplish were still there. We could still get them. We knew we were down but we weren't out.

Besides the losses and the way my hand was hurting, I was also getting a lot of criticism. During the year, I'd scored eighty-six runs, and now I was thinking, I'm the leadoff guy. This is on me. And I was hearing that again: *Pedroia, you suck!*

I took the attitude, "Okay, the train's coming, and when you see it, don't jump on because you should have a long time ago." I believe that I approach things in a way that works over the long haul and makes me successful. The way I prepare for games, and the way I play, has always led to success. I was telling people who were criticizing me, "Don't kick me while I'm down. You can get on me a little, but don't kick me."

In Game Five we faced Sabathia again. In this game, I got two hits. I doubled to lead off the seventh and scored when Youk tripled. Youk had a great game, Manny and Mike Lowell homered, and we won 7-1 to put the series at 3-2. So we were alive. We were coming back to Boston, with Schill pitching Game Six. I thought, He ain't losing, no way. He won't allow it. People can say what they want about Curt Schilling, but there's one guy you want on the mound when you have to win—and we have a few guys like that on our team.

Schill went out there, took the ball, and did what he did. I mean, he *shoved*. We got four runs in the first inning, and six in the third, and he left with us up 10-2. Then we got two more and won 12-2, to tie the series.

GAME SEVEN. I'D never been a part of a Game Seven, and that feeling where you know only one team is going on after tonight. Either I was going back to Arizona after the game, which would totally suck, or we'd be staying right there and playing in the World Series.

Dice-K was pitching and in the top of the first he put them down one-two-three.

I led off the bottom of the first. The place was electric.

I hit a single to left field, and people were going nuts.

We got single runs in the first, second, and third. In the fourth inning I came up for my third at-bat, with men on first and third. I hit a bullet up the middle, but Asdrubal Cabrera was playing right there and turned it for a double play. I was thinking, You gotta be shitting me. A one-run lead in the playoffs wasn't enough. Every run is huge in the playoffs. If you're not one swing away, then you have to get a guy on and then hit the bomb.

Cleveland scored a run in the top of the fourth and one in the top of the fifth. I came up in the seventh with the score still 3-2. Jacoby Ellsbury had gotten to second when he hit a ground ball and the Indians' third baseman, Casey Blake, made an error on the throw to first. Then Jacoby moved to third on a sacrifice bunt by Julio Lugo.

Rafael Betancourt was pitching. He throws the high fastball, and I hit high fastballs well. So I was thinking, Cool.

Waiting on deck, I had been thinking about the times in the past I'd gone up against Betancourt. The first time I'd been up against him in this series was Game Two, with two outs in the ninth inning—and I'd gotten a hit off him on a high fastball. It was a line drive to left field. Before that, I remembered facing him one other time in Cleveland, and he'd thrown me a ball that kind of cut. I was thinking about this as I waited in the on-deck circle. I thought that if the pitch was up, I might get a chance to get a little under it and lift it to the outfield. I was taking my practice swings thinking specifically about that.

As I walked to the plate, my mind-set was to look for that four-seam fastball, belt high, because I knew I could get around on it. I was thinking it would be coming in at ninety-four or ninety-five miles per hour, but I was confident my hands were quick enough to catch up to that pitch.

I was digging into the batter's box thinking, Okay, if I can hit a fly ball we can get Jacoby in . . . I knew the infield would be playing in, and I was telling myself to just get it into the outfield somehow.

Betancourt wound up and threw. He gave me that perfect high fastball on the first pitch and I swung and fouled it straight back.

I was thinking, Shit! That was it! That was the one. It was like this feeling of grief, that it was there for you, and now it's passed you by. It was my first postseason and I didn't really know what to think. Jacoby was right down that third-base line. The pitch had been right there! I should have crushed it!

I stepped out of the box and got refocused. I cinched up my batting gloves and dug back in. I knew Jacoby was stepping off third base behind me, stretching out a lead. The infield was dropping down now, creeping in. I suspected I might see the other pitch, the one that cut, and I was thinking, Just hit a fly ball now. Just get that run in. Just get it in the air.

At that point in the game, one run would seem like ten.

Then I thought, But if he does throw that high fastball again, this time I'm gonna put that bitch onto the Mass. Turnpike.

Betancourt, a right-hander, looked at Jacoby on third, turned his head back to me, and threw the pitch. It was the high fastball. Just as he let it go, my head was saying, This shit is about to go very far. I swung and as it came off the bat, my next thought was, We're going to the World Series . . . This is all over.

That feeling was unbelievable. The minute I hit that ball the crowd went nuts. That roar, in a moment like that, hits you from behind like a wind. As the ball went over the Green Monster, the noise was so loud it felt like it all hadn't really just happened. It all felt so fast that I was probably past second base before it felt like this was a real thing, happening right now.

We were up 5-2.

In the eighth inning I came up with the bases loaded and two outs, and I doubled to center to clear the bases to put it out of reach. We won 11-2. We were going to the World Series. In the end, I'd gone 5 for 9 in Games Six and Seven, and finished the series with a .345 average.

THE FIRST TWO games of the 2007 World Series were incredible. The Colorado Rockies had just swept the Diamondbacks in the National League Championship Series, and they'd been resting up for six days. We'd just fought back from elimination. The Rockies came into Fenway ready to kick our asses. But it was going to be our year.

In the first inning, Josh Beckett looked unbeatable, striking out the side.

Then I led off the bottom of the first inning against Jeff Francis. He had gone 17-9 that year during the regular season, and he'd pitched a 5-1 win against Arizona in the NLCS.

His first pitch was a little outside, and then his second was a fastball low. I leaned in and swung, launching it just over the Green Monster. Later, somebody told me it was only the second home run in history to lead off a World Series. Don Buford had done it for the Orioles in the 1969 World Series against the Mets. I was the first rookie ever to do it.

I really didn't think anything about it. I thought my home run in the ALCS against Cleveland was a lot bigger than that home run. I know leading off with it gave us the lead, but the home run in the ALCS helped us pull off that comeback. The World Series was just fun. I didn't feel nervous at all during the Series, which is weird.

Meanwhile, Beckett was pitching on eight days of rest, so he was throwing it, like, 150 miles an hour. When Josh is in the playoffs, he tones it up. He's a different man.

After that home run, we just boat-raced them. It ended up 13-1.

When we came out the next day, Schill was shoving. Obviously, it wasn't the best stuff he's ever had—it was late in his career, and his arm was probably hurting him, but there's not a pitcher like him in that situation. After allowing one run in the first inning, he pitched into the sixth, scattering four hits and striking out four.

To beat the Rockies 2-1 the way Schill did, given the Rockies' offense, was tremendous.

We went out to Denver for Game Three, and that's when I had trouble getting into the stadium.

We got there, and I was all fired up to play. I was totally locked in, thinking about how we were two games away from a World Championship. I was thinking, We're the best team *ever*. That's what you think, getting ready to play.

I was walking into the players' gate at Coors Field, and this guy barks at me: "Hey, you got your ID?"

Yeah, I had my ID, and I showed it to him. He looked at it really closely, then looked at me.

"This isn't you," he said.

I was thinking, Well, who the f— is it, then? But I was trying to be respectful. So I said, "Yeah, that's me."

"Anybody can make fake IDs," he said.

Now I was starting to get pissed. "Dude, are you serious? No offense, but I'm here to play in the World Series." I didn't need this right now.

"Well," the guy said, "I'm calling security."

I said to him, "You don't know who I am? You don't know who I am? Ask Jeff Francis who I am!"

Then I pushed past him. Tito was standing there, laughing.

When I got to the clubhouse, I was still angry. I was wondering if they were serious, or just doing that to piss me off and distract me. But I also knew we had one job to do: win two games and get the hell out of Denver.

In Game Three, we just kept on going. Jacoby got four hits, and I got three hits. It felt great that the two youngest players on the team were contributing in a real way. In Boston, it's usually the veteran guys who have been through this who deliver. I think Jacoby and I were playing with blinders on. We were just playing like we had no fear. It was as if we couldn't screw up, and if we did, who cared? What are you going to say: a twenty-three-year-old kid screwed up? No shit, we didn't know any better. With Dice-K pitching, we won 10-5.

GAME FOUR WAS one of those games where you just want it to be over: We had all come this far. We were one win away. How was it going to end? The night before, trying to sleep, I kept playing everything in my mind. And then in the game itself, watching in the ninth inning when Jacoby made an unbelievable catch on a drive to left by Jamey Carroll for the second out, and seeing Jonathan Papelbon on the mound with just one out to go, I kept thinking, It just has to end now. I was thinking, Jon Lester has pitched into the sixth to get us here, and he's just beaten cancer. This can't not happen.

And I was out there, and it was all going through my head, and everybody's family was there, and then Papelbon was in his windup, and throwing, and Seth Smith was swinging, and missing, and it was over. It was ours. It was a couple of minutes after midnight back in Boston and I was thinking that people must be going nuts back there.

Winning the World Series was a different feeling than what I expected. It had been so hard getting by the Indians in the ALCS. That had seemed like a nonstop battle. The last pitch in Denver, when Smith swung and Pap's fastball went past him, seemed like one of those moments where it's over but you don't really know it yet. Being down three games to one against Cleveland, with the team right at the brink of being eliminated, my mind was set on one thing: *the season can't end*, and I had put everything into that objective. Now, twelve days later, we were World Champs but my mind was still saying *don't let the season end*. We had all been fighting so hard, we didn't care where or what or how—we just wanted to win every pitch.

Seth Smith swung and missed; I was thinking, Oh, shit, what do I do now?

Some of us really didn't know what to do. Guys who had been on the 2004 team—Ortiz, Manny, Wakefield, and Varitek among them—had been here before. But most of us hadn't.

Seth Smith swung and missed; everybody was running to Pap.

It was all happening so fast. A second before, I had been standing there watching Smith get himself ready, pointing the end of his bat at the mound for a long pause before bringing it up behind him, watching Pap go into his windup on a pitch that could win us the World Series, and time felt as if it had slowed down to a crawl. There they were, pitcher and batter: Pap wanting to close it out, Smith wanting in any way he could to do what we had wanted to do so badly in Cleveland—not let the season end, not now, not here.

Seth Smith swung and missed; time seemed like it was suddenly rushing by.

We ran to the mound, all of us from every position, from the dugout, from the bullpen, all together into a mass of people. But what I remember is not so much what I was doing, but what I was thinking: I can't believe we did it. I can't believe we did it. We'd been one game from Cleveland ending it for us. Everyone had written us off.

We had beaten the Rockies handily. That was where we really played great baseball. Our pitching and defense was phenomenal. We got huge hits. It was one of those things where every single thing we did, for the last seven games of the season, we did exactly right. There wasn't one thing that went wrong. It was nearly perfect baseball.

I thought, This is over. We don't have to fight through anything else. We don't have to overcome the next thing. We don't have to have the pressure of playing for a World Championship on us anymore. But I also thought, This has been the most incredible stretch of baseball in our lives, when every guy on the team had to come together and do everything possible for the success of the team, and now it's come to its end.

THAT NIGHT, THE three Red Sox owners threw a party for us at the hotel. Everybody was there, all the players and their families. It was a huge party, but it was different than what you'd expect. Everybody was tired, because of how hard we played for so long, and it was a quiet kind of satisfaction we were experiencing. I think I had one beer, and I went to bed at two in the morning. It wasn't like we stayed up and partied all night. Everybody was happy, but also mentally and physically drained from the season, the grind, and the pressure. Everything had hit us all at once. I was exhausted. The next morning, we got up at 8 A.M. and flew back to Boston, where people were going absolutely crazy. I hadn't known what to expect. The whole season had been like that for me. You're a rookie, you're going through everything, and you're learning as you go. Now you've just won the World Series. People had signs everywhere.

The day after we flew back, October 30, was the "Rolling Rally," a parade where we went through the city riding on amphibious World War II–style DUCK boats. It was amazing how the city embraced us. There were thousands of fans all along the three-mile parade route.

It was a chance for me to really take a step back, in a way you can't do when you're on the field and locked in on the game, and really look at the fans, to really see their faces and get a sense of who they are.

The Boston fans love the Red Sox and they should. The Red Sox are a bunch of guys who love to play baseball. They're hardworking, blue-collar players who enjoy playing the game and will do anything to help the Red Sox win. I think the fans realize that, and it's what makes the whole Red Sox Nation so big. There are players any fan can relate to. If you look up and down our lineup I'm sure any fan can pick out one guy and say, "That guy's my favorite player. I love Kevin Youkilis because of the way he plays and the look on his face when he makes an out." Or "I love Josh Beckett because of the fire in him and the way he looks on the mound and how intimidating he is."

They might like Ellsbury because of his speed and athleticism and how fun and exciting he is. Mike Lowell—what is there not to like about him? The guy is a true professional. He's a guy who had to beat cancer and come back. A first-class man.

I think there's a certain player every fan can relate to and that's what makes our team so special. And that's what makes it so special for the fans. They identify the guy they love and that guy will be their favorite player forever.

WHO WOULD HAVE believed it: here was a World Series title three years after the 2004 Series, a victory people had waited their whole lifetimes to see. The fans looked like kids who had just been handed a second piece of birthday cake. It was a happy day for a lot of people, and for us.

It felt great, too, that so many younger guys had contributed. Jacoby had a great series, Jon Lester had done what he did, coming back from cancer and then winning Game Four of a World Series, and even Youk, who had been on the 2004 World Series roster without playing much, this time had been such a huge part of how this season had gone. And it was the veterans who had helped us all come along. As you go through 162 games and then the post-season, players fight through injuries, players go through stuff personally, but they help each other out. That's the best thing about the season: not the winning streaks or the losing streaks, but just dealing with the grind. When you're on that Red Sox team, your teammates always have your back.

A guy along the parade route had a huge sign that was so funny, we actually took it from him. In the picture, Big Papi has a baby carrier, with me in it! It was a spoof on the poster from the movie *Little Man*. That sign is still hanging in Tito's office at Fenway Park.

There were so many excited kids on the parade route.

I like it if the kids who watch me play baseball can say, "This is what it's about—this guy's out there having a really great time, just playing the game, enjoying being around his teammates and the fans." I hope they see that when they watch me. Because that's what I did back when I was their age.

I remember how much fun baseball was when I was a kid. I'd get home from school in the afternoon and have a Little League game to look forward to at seven o'clock, under the lights. I'd think, Just like the major leaguers do . . .

I'd get home and put my uniform on and sit for hours, waiting until my parents would take me to the game. I hope kids still have that passion for baseball that I did. If I wasn't playing in a game that day, I'd go to a game just to watch. There were games every single night of the week. I was always at the field. They had a main field, where the game was being played, and they had a back field with no lights, where guys would bring their bats and gloves and we'd just start playing. There would be just enough light from the floodlights on the big field for us to see by, and so we'd go back there and play and play. Even now, when I get into a slump or some other rut, I try to take myself back to when I was a kid, playing out there in the dark, just doing it because it was fun, and nothing more. We were just these shapes in the dark, playing, swinging at balls we could barely see, keeping at it until our parents came for us and made us come on home.

WHAT A YEAR 2007 was, with all that had happened. There had been the early-season craziness of Dice-K signing with the team and coming to Boston, then my struggles early on, then injuries to Schill and Wakefield, then their coming back stronger and all of us accomplishing our goal as a team. And Jacoby coming up from the minors and playing so well. There were so many things, so many twists and turns.

It had been nearly nine months of going hard and dealing with different things, and now it was here. We were World Champions. It was one of the greatest feelings ever. And it was something no one could ever change and that you never had to give back.

Julia Ruth Stevens

Red Sox Fan

I live in Arizona in the winter, but I spend every summer in Conway, New Hampshire, where I've lived for sixty years. And I love watching the Red Sox. I'm ninety-two now, and I'm legally blind, but I have special glasses I use to watch the games on the television.

I used to be a Yankees fan, but some years ago I switched over to the Red Sox. I've lived in New Hampshire so long that I became attached to the Boston team. I don't think Daddy would have minded. After all, he started out in the major leagues with the Red Sox.

I switched to the Red Sox and then some time later, they finally won the World Series. Some people asked me if they thought that the Curse had been lifted because I was Babe Ruth's daughter, and I had switched my teams. But I don't think so—it's just a good story to tell because there never really was a curse. After all, being traded to the Yankees and playing the outfield full-time was what really established Daddy's career. If I remember correctly, the Curse actually was a clever idea that a sportswriter dreamed up.

I switched because I like the way the Red Sox play. They play the game as it should be played, like a team. And they play very hard.

I like the little second baseman, Dustin Pedroia. He plays like they did in the old days. It's a pleasure to watch them play hard. When my husband was alive, we'd watch the Red Sox on the television, and when they'd get behind, he'd say, "Looks like it's all over... I'm going to bed..." But I'd stay up until the end of the game, and you know what? Lots of times they would come back and win the game. And in the morning, I'd say to him, "You went to bed too early—don't ever count the Red Sox out!"

I used to like Johnny Damon, before he went off to play with the Yankees. I would have preferred that he stayed with the Red Sox. But at least if you go to play for the Yankees, they make you get your hair cut. I can't say I disagreed with that! I think ballplayers should look like ballplayers, the way they did in the old days. A good haircut is very important for a ballplayer.

I was sorry when the Red Sox didn't make the World Series last year, after coming so close. But I think they'll do it again. As I say, they have a team of good young men who know how the game should be played.

That's why I like to watch the second baseman, Pedroia. He plays the game very hard. He's always trying his best. There's something about the way he plays that's very nice. And he can hit the ball!

Yes, I really like that second baseman. But if you want to know the truth, my favorite player of all is Papelbon. I think he's fascinating, and I love to watch him. Now he's really something, that Papelbon!

14

Rookie of the Year

On November 12, two weeks into the off-season, I got the call telling me I'd been named American League Rookie of the Year. After the way the year had started out, and after the way I had struggled through so much, the news was sweet. It had been very tough on my wife, and really on my whole family, to start out playing as badly as I had; by now I felt I had proved everybody wrong, and had proved that I did belong in the big leagues, in Boston with the Red Sox.

We went to the New York Hilton in January so I could receive the award at the Baseball Writers' dinner. It was really a memorable night. Kelli and my parents were there, and I sat with Willie Randolph, the Mets' manager, and pitcher C. C. Sabathia. I was presented the award by Craig Biggio, who was retiring as second baseman of the Astros after playing twenty seasons in the big leagues; I had admired him for years, especially because he played his entire career for one team.

When I got up in front of that New York crowd, I said, "Thank you for not booing me." They liked that.

When we were leaving the dinner, I told Kelli how awesome the evening had been. I said I'd love to come back sometime, if it were ever possible.

She said, "Oh, we'll be here next year."

I told her the only way that could happen is if I was named Most Valuable Player.

"I know," she said.

That winter, everything was fun. The holidays with the family were great, and then I went to the Baseball Writers' dinner in Boston in January and met all kinds of people I never thought I'd have a chance to meet. Three players from the 1967 Red Sox—Jim Lonborg, Rico Petrocelli, and Russ Gibson—were being honored that night.

It was great to celebrate having been on the biggest stage, and succeeding there. But it didn't take away from the fact that I had set my sights on being a better player than I'd ever been before. My goal was not to win one championship, but to continue to win championships for the Red Sox.

My plan after we won the World Series was to clear my head and go right back to square one with my conditioning and preparation.

The day I got back to Arizona, I went to the best hand surgeon in the country, Dr. Donald Sheridan in Scottsdale. I was fortunate he was right there in Arizona. They did a bone scan and an MRI on the hand, and when he looked at the results and saw the crack in it, he said, "You're lucky. That hand was just about to crumble."

I said, "What does that mean?"

He said, "That means if it had happened, you're not playing."

I'd made it through. I had the surgery the next day and everything went well. I had a cast on for a while as it healed.

Kelli and I bought a house in Arizona a few miles away from the condo we had. It was out in the country, out in the desert.

So, I was married, my wife and I had just bought a house, and my baseball team had just won the World Series. I felt like an adult.

We had to move all our stuff to the new house, but because of the hand, I couldn't even pick up a box. So Kelli did everything. But the day after the surgery, I was at Athletes' Performance, lifting with just my legs.

I'd always felt that my legs had never fully recovered from that injury I had when I was a freshman in high school, that they had never gotten strong enough. I'd been a lot faster before I broke my leg. When I was in seventh and eighth grade I used to fly. No, not like Jacoby Ellsbury, but I could run well. That injury really set me back. Now I had the opportunity to work on making my lower body as strong as my upper body had become.

It was January, and it was "Here we go; here comes 2008." I was getting ready.

Every off-season I take the same approach: I have another job, and that's working out. Baseball's done, so I have to go and get in my workouts. My wife yells at me that I have to take a little time off. But that winter I worked out on Thanksgiving Day, and Christmas Day, and New Year's Day. But I do that because the whole time I'm thinking, No one else is. That's how I get my edge. That's why in game 161, I'll be better than I was in game ten.

I HAD TEN weeks where I couldn't work on my upper body. I did so much running I felt like I could run a marathon. Then I began working on my shoulders, and then the cast came off and I could work on my arms. It felt like it was all coming together at just the right time.

In the winter before the 2008 season, I was joined at Athletes' Performance by two of my teammates, Youk and Manny. Manny usually worked out in Florida in the off-season, but he spent three months at the Arizona facility getting ready to go. The workouts included lifting, sprinting with weighted sleds, flexibility, and agility drills. There were guys from other teams there, too—Nomar Garciaparra was there, and Nick Punto from the Twins. Working out with someone like Carl Crawford of the Tampa Bay Rays made me realize how much harder I had to work to get quicker and more agile.

I tried to have fun even when working out. I was definitely the jokester. I warned them about how dangerous it is to get in the way of my rockets. I told them I didn't want them getting hurt. There are football players who work out at Athletes' Performance, and they'd be walking around completely jacked, and I'd ask them when they were getting on their Jenny Craig diets. One humongous guy was always talking shit at me. So I did a set of bench presses, ripped off my shirt, and threw it at him. He started popping off. He said, "Who the hell is that little white guy?"

Somebody said, "That's the Rookie of the Year."

"That guy? I thought he was in high school . . ."

I was ready to kick his ass right there. Or maybe I was just ready to attempt to.

During my two-a-days before the 2007 season, Brady Quinn, now a quarterback for the Cleveland Browns, was there. He'd just finished playing quarterback at Notre Dame and was getting ready for the draft. He came walking by while I was playing Ping-Pong, and I was kicking somebody's ass. He was looking at me, walking all slow like he was tough. I just perked up.

I said, "Hey, buddy, you don't know shit yet. You played at Notre Dame with that cupcake schedule you guys are rolling out these days. Walk on and keep your mouth shut, or pick up the paddle."

He was probably thinking, Who the hell is this midget who's talking shit at me?

The next day he comes by and says he wants to get on the table.

I said, "Dude, before you come on, just remember this is serious shit, this isn't just Notre Dame spring practice. This is *serious* shit." I was getting him all fired up.

He grabbed the paddle, and I beat the living shit out of him. He got beaten like he'd never been beaten in his life. We were using Halex Ping-Pong balls, and I swear he walked off with the word *Halex* imprinted on places all over his body. I was talking trash at him, telling him, "You have to be mentally tough to play Ping-Pong around here, dude. You've got to get tougher, Brady." So of course, we became friends—in a shit-talking, I'll-kick-your-ass kind of way. I'd see him every day and scream at him to get him a little tougher.

Those football guys, they're hilarious to be around, because they're so ridiculously big. They're also relaxed, because I think their season beats them up so bad that in their off-season workouts they feel like they can just chill and get it done.

Everybody just laughed at me when I was talking shit. I gave Carl Crawford so much of it, that after a while he just shook his head and didn't bother saying anything back.

• • •

I TRY TO have fun working out, but I look at the off-season as a time to build up enough stamina to last eight months. I watch everything I eat, and I'm working out all the time. In the season, you're maintaining the fitness for eight months. In the off-season, you have three months to make the most gain possible, to become better.

In the off-season I get up every morning right at 7 A.M., and I have my strict eating regimen, right from 7 A.M. until I go to bed at 10 P.M. For my workout, I'm pretty much doing the same thing every day. I leave the house at 7:30 A.M. and get home about 4:15 P.M. It's a long day—a full-time job. People figure we go home in the off-season and just relax. I'm sure some guys do that. But not me. I do everything I can to prepare to play 162 games, and possibly nineteen more in the playoffs.

It's about being as ready as you can be. No, you can't control the freak injuries, but you might have some control over the little ones. You don't want to have a pulled hamstring or a quad injury in the season because you didn't work hard on flexibility when you could. In 2008 I played in 157 regular-season games and eleven more in the postseason.

I train mentally, too. You have to do that to have what it takes in the big leagues.

In my final year at Arizona State, I had 244 at-bats. In the major leagues, you can have 350 at-bats and still be in June—I ended up with 653 at-bats in the 2008 season. That's where the mental aspect comes in. The season is *long*. You need to show up at the ballpark every day being ready to play and ready to win. I don't sit back and say, "I'll need to go 20 for 60 to get to .300." That's not the way I tick. The way I tick is that if I'm up in the eighth inning in a tight game, and one that could be late in the season, I don't care if I'm 0 for 4 or 4 for 4, I just need to get on base to help our team win. I don't care if I hit a ground ball right to the second baseman and he completely misses it to allow me on. If I'm standing on first base, I've done my job.

Another month, and it was the start of another season.

Fred Lynn

Boston Red Sox Center Fielder 1974–80

American League Rookie of the Year, 1975

American League Most Valuable Player, 1975

The difference between my second year and just about every-body else's in baseball was that while my first year was unique—winning Rookie of the Year and Most Valuable Player—my second year was unique as well, because I also played that year unsigned. A big free agency case was going to the courts, and my agent had me not sign a one-year contract until that case was completed. I had a lot of things going on in my second year that no one else had. But coming off a better-than-expected rookie year creates pressure for anyone.

For Dustin, after what he accomplished in his rookie year, it was a matter of going out and trying to do more. You don't just want to stay status quo, even if you've had a great year.

But I didn't see that in Dustin's makeup, that he would have been trying to stay status quo. He seemed like the kind of kid who was not going to allow himself to fail—it just was not an option for him. He didn't seem the type to fall into a malaise where he'd get too comfortable or satisfied with what he was doing, or what he had already accomplished. He seems like someone who will always strive for bigger and better things. He's got that little chip on his shoulder that's good to have in pro sports.

I saw that kind of attitude in a teammate of mine with the Red Sox. Rick Burleson was the team's shortstop from 1974 to 1980. "The Rooster." He was a very similar style of player. He was a very scrappy guy, the kind of player who would fight you in a second.

Rooster used to have a big swing. He tried to hit home runs, even though he wasn't that big a guy. He had that same attitude of "I'm not that big a guy, but I'm still going to hit it over the fence."

But Rooster found out, a couple of years in, that hitting this way wasn't where the money was for him. He was a right-handed hitter, but he discovered right field. That's when he became a really good hitter, especially first and second in the lineup, because he could move guys over. He could get hits, and sometimes he'd pop one out of the park.

Now with Dustin, on the other hand, he's got a bit more sock because he's got a really big swing. He generates a lot of power. I'm not going to say he's a little man, I'm going to say he's a man who is not that tall. I don't think he's that little; I think he's pretty well built. I haven't seen him in the locker room, but on the field he looks like a little fireplug.

Dustin does go off into these little tailspins where he doesn't hit, but the important thing is that he always knows he can hit. That sense never leaves him. He has hit well at every level, and even when he came to the big leagues and was scuffling a bit, he knew in his heart that he could hit—and do it in his own way.

His way is to just go up there and hack. He's fun to watch.

With that swing, Dustin generates some serious power, and he will hit some home runs. But at first I wondered if when he started trying to hit home runs—when he would try to put balls over the left-field wall—he might start having some problems. I felt that as long as he used the whole field, instead of trying too much to hit home runs, he'd be just fine.

But when I first saw him swing, I said, "Whoa."

Because when I first saw him with that big swing, he was hitting about a buck-thirty, and I thought, Well, I don't know . . . I didn't know about his minor-league or college career and all his successes at those levels. I saw this small kid with this big swing, and I thought, He may want to cut that down a little bit.

When he was going into his second season, he had challenges.

Your first year in the majors, every pitcher you see, every hotel you stay in, every ballpark you visit, it's a new experience. You're constantly out of your comfort zone. You're learning. Everything is exciting, and it keeps you motivated.

The second year, a couple of things happen. First of all, you've seen the pitchers and the hotels and the ballparks. Secondly, the league is now going to make an adjustment to you. You've proved to them you can hit. You've shown them you can hit this pitch or that pitch. Now they're going to come at you differently. It's like, "What you saw from me last year, you're not going to see from me this year."

A guy coming out of a strong rookie season is going to have to make an adjustment, because everybody in the league is making an adjustment to him. And when they do, they may find a weakness. A team may say, "There are three pitchers who all pitch this way, and they all get him out." The word will then travel throughout the league. If it's the case that he can be pitched to in a certain way, if it's the case that there's just this little hole in his game, they will find it. Then he's got to figure out how to make the adjustment back.

In my playing days, the pitchers and catchers and coaches figured it out with their heads. Now it's also computers, where they can compute pitching patterns. If they find that Roy Halladay can get Pedroia out with fastballs, there's a chart on that. The chart may say to pitch fastball, fastball, slider. We didn't have computers; we had pitchers and catchers who figured it out. Because either way, they will figure it out.

The second year is usually when that all gets worked out. Some players can adjust, and some can't. And sometimes a player doesn't need to adjust. Sometimes, just sometimes, he might not have that hole they're looking for.

15

Establishing a Routine

It was a weird deal, the way we started the 2008 season. Having won the World Series in 2007, everyone was excited that our whole team was returning the next season. But everyone was also tired. Our season had ended on October 28, so we were already looking at an off-season a month shorter than most other teams'— not that we were complaining about that.

But then the phone rang early in November: we might be heading to Japan to open the 2008 season, doing so earlier than other teams because of that.

My first thought was, That's going to be pretty difficult on our pitching staff.

Going that extra month the season before, and starting something like a month early the following year, meant there would not be a lot of downtime. The position players can handle it, because your body recovers pretty quickly. But it's tough on our pitchers. They really need recovery time for their arms.

The Yankees had done that at the beginning of the 2004 season, when they went to Japan to open against the Rays. They later said it made for a long season.

Once we found out we were going, spring training was a bit like "Hurry up, let's get ready and play two [regular-season] games, wait a week, and then start our season." Yes, it would be fun to travel to Japan, to see their culture. But on the other hand I worried it would hurt our team and how we prepared to accomplish our goals. After all, we were the defending champions and felt we could go back and win the World Series again.

WHEN I GOT to spring training, I was in what I felt was the best shape of my life. I'd raised that level even from the beginning of the 2007 season.

But I don't set individual goals. Winning another championship is all that really matters. And so in Fort Myers, we all had one goal, which was to try to repeat.

That spring, I was now a teammate, not just a guy trying to make it into the lineup. I knew the guys, and they knew me. Manny and I continued to build a relationship. He saw the way I played and had fun seeing a young kid enjoy baseball so much. Manny's a big kid himself. He loves to play baseball. Baseball is my life; that's all I know. I think Manny admired that and started to respect me, rather than just looking at me as a rookie, a young guy.

His locker was in the back of the clubhouse at City of Palms Park, along with guys like Ortiz, Lugo, and Sean Casey. My locker was nearby. He walked over with a bat over his shoulder and a gift-wrapped box in his hand, and just handed it to me.

I started taking off the wrapping paper, and I saw the word *Rolex* on the box. Just as I did, Manny smashed his bat into the box, putting this big dent in it.

When he did that, I figured it was just a joke. Manny was always doing crazy things. It was just another Manny goof.

But I opened the box, and it really was a Rolex watch, and it still worked! I suddenly remembered the summer before, when he'd told me that if I won Rookie of the Year and batted over .300 he'd buy me a watch. Now he was following through on that. And he'd written a nice note to congratulate me.

I thought, Damn. He smashed a twenty-thousand-dollar watch that he just gave me, with his bat. Is this guy crazy?

Then Manny went wandering off. Why he would take his bat and smash a really expensive Rolex he was giving me? I still have no idea.

I GOT SEVEN hits in spring training. That was two more hits than last year's, to make my spring training batting average a cool .140. Sweet!

I always tell our hitting coach Dave Magadan, who works with me for hours, that I don't care if I'm playing in a Wiffle ball game, I always want to rake.

He said, "It takes time to get back into it. You're young, you'll learn. You're going to be fine."

SPRING TRAINING IN 2008 also had some funny moments. One was when the Mike Lowell Foundation hosted a "Dancing with the All-Stars" event. I agreed to dance in it, even though I can't dance at all (not even a little).

Mike has done great work with his charity. Like Jon Lester and my wife, he's a cancer survivor, having had a bout with testicular cancer in 1999. Mike and his wife, Bertha, started the foundation a couple of years later to help children with cancer.

The event was on a Saturday night at a hotel in Bonita Springs. The Red Sox who danced were Mike, Alex Cora, Jonathan Papelbon, and myself. We were each paired with a professional dancer who spent a couple of hours trying to teach us some basic steps for dances, such as the merengue and the salsa. And everybody knows that Pap can dance, loves to dance, and has been pretty much a dancing legend since the 2007 season.

I'm probably the worst dancer ever.

Team owner John Henry was in attendance, as was Tito, who was giving me a hard time.

I said, "Hey Tito, what if I ripped off my shirt and threw it at John Henry's head?"

Tito said, "That would be the funniest thing I have ever seen in my life."

I told him, "You know what? I'm going to do it."

I wanted to get this crowd going, especially since we all looked like idiots dancing, especially me and Pap. Now, we had Mike Lowell and Alex Cora, who are Latino, so they had some experience and at least looked okay when they danced. But then you had Pap and me. Basically, we couldn't even move. Pap is much better with the Dropkick Murphys rocking behind him, as they did during the World Series parade, when the band whose song plays when he enters a game was onstage with him.

Before we started, Mike Lowell said, "Let's write something on your chest."

I said, "Whatever, dude."

He wrote "Daddy." I have no idea why. It was hilarious. People were shooting video of it, and it ended up all over the Internet, including on YouTube.

As I was dancing with my partner, I just went for it and ripped my shirt off. It was a button shirt, so it ripped pretty good. Then I threw it at John Henry, but it missed him and hit some lady who was sitting behind him in the head, which made it even funnier. Tito was laughing so hard he almost wet his pants. It was just one of those nights.

WE OPENED THE 2008 season in Japan. The team had finished spring training united in a lot of ways, including when we threatened to boycott an exhibition game against Toronto to be sure the Red Sox coaches were going to be compensated for the Japan trip, as the players were.

But once that was settled, we were on our way. We arrived in Japan after an eighteen-hour trip. That was an experience. Not only had we brought in a lot of fans from New England, but the Japanese fans were crazed. It was in Tokyo that I realized Dice-K actually *was* Elvis Presley. At the concession stands, they were selling Dice-K Red Sox jerseys for something like three hundred dollars. Dice-K, he was the man there, the biggest thing in sports. Everyone was drawn to him. He's got that funny personality.

It was an amazing scene in the Tokyo Dome when Dice-K came out, a million flashbulbs going off as he pitched that first game. It seemed like it was the Oakland A's versus the whole country of Japan that day, not just the Red Sox. "Sweet Caroline" played in the eighth inning, just as it does at Fenway. The Japanese fans were doing cheers like what you'd see at a college football game. It was weird, and it was fun.

The Tokyo Dome was jammed for our games. First we played an exhibition against the Hanshin Tigers, then opened against the A's. It was the earliest opening game in the history of the major leagues, so we knew it was going to be a long season. But it started out on the right note. Dice-K left in the fifth with us behind by a run, but by the sixth inning the game was tied 4-4. I doubled off Joe Blanton, then Youk walked, and then Manny doubled to score both of us. Dice-K didn't get the win for the Japanese fans, but it turned out that Hideki Okajima, our relief pitcher who had played for the Yomiuri Giants (the team that uses the Tokyo Dome as its home field), got the win instead. That was a good ending to the night.

The downside was, as I said, that we were starting the year much earlier than other teams, and there was the travel to and from Japan in just a few days. All of that was really tough on our pitching staff. We were playing games when our bodies were telling us it was six o'clock in the morning. We split the two games in Tokyo with the Oakland Athletics, then flew back to Los Angeles for an exhibition against the Dodgers at the L.A. Coliseum before we played the A's again in Oakland. At the Coliseum, the field dimensions were even smaller than when the Dodgers first played there back in 1959; the left-field screen was something like two hundred feet from home plate, and the screen was sixty feet high. The Dodgers didn't even use a left fielder, but had a five-man infield. It was fun, and different, and in a way it all added to the feeling of being totally disoriented.

HOW DO I feel about old versus new ballparks? Well, obviously, Fenway isn't the newest place in the world and that's probably its only negative. The atmosphere, the fans, the dimensions of the field and the Green Monster—Fenway has a great feel to it. I've never seen anybody come into Fenway Park and say, "This place sucks." In my mind it's the best stadium in the world.

You have your new ballparks, too, such as Arizona, Houston, Cincinnati, and Philly. Those ballparks are built for the players. You go inside the clubhouse and they have TVs everywhere, couches everywhere, reclining chairs. In Houston the seats are comfortable and close to the field, with great sight lines. What an unbelievably fan-friendly ballpark that is.

Either way, the different types of ballparks you play in are another thing that makes the game so special. We'll be on a road trip and say, "Where are we heading today? Seattle! Cool." You can see out of their half-dome. No matter where we are, though, I feel comfortable in the clubhouse, getting ready to play. The more often I go to each city, the more it feels like a routine.

IT'S A LONG season when you play in the major leagues. When the first few games go by, everyone gets into whatever routine works for them. Me, I practically live at the ballpark. Everybody has a routine that gets them comfortable and helps them focus. Mine just might be a little more stretched out. But in the 2008 season, I had developed a daily routine that worked for me. A lot of it went back to my summer playing ball in Carson City.

A lot of people ask about my routine, so here's what I settled on in 2008 for home games:

On game days, I'd get up at about eleven in the morning. Kelli would cook me a huge breakfast. I eat the same breakfast every day. I have two eggs, two protein waffles, two pieces of bacon, and two oranges. I have a glass of orange juice with that. I don't exactly know why I do that—the "two of each thing" deal doesn't have anything to do with anything. It's just how much I eat. It's not superstitious—eating two of each thing isn't going to make me get two hits in the game.

After I ate, I would shower and get dressed. At 12:15 or so I would sit on our couch by the window of the apartment, where I could see down the block to the players' gate. We lived on the tenth floor of a building one block from Fenway. In my head, I'd be thinking, I'm ready to f—— go, but I'd be waiting for the gate to open. I'd put ESPN *First Take* on the TV and sit there for almost exactly forty-five minutes, watching TV and constantly glancing down the street at the gate, waiting for the fun.

Then the gate would open. I'd be up off the couch and heading to our door.

"Kelli, I'm going . . ."

"Okay . . . good luck!"

Even though it was an easy walk to the field, I would usually end up driving because some fans might get a little out of control. At 12:50 I would drive over there, and park my car in the players' lot, and head into the clubhouse.

Coming into the clubhouse always felt good. It would be quiet, and I could start thinking about that night's game and what I needed to do. At one o'clock, I would always play a couple of games of cribbage with Tito. Usually, we were the only two people in the clubhouse at that point.

The cribbage began one time when, hours before a game, Tito must have been bored. He came at me and pretty much just told me we were playing cribbage.

Tito and I began playing, and that became another part of the routine. I played with other guys, like Mike Lowell.

I'm even competitive in cribbage. During June, the Red Sox were on a Fox Network telecast, and Fox had us each do an ID of ourselves to be used in the broadcast. I ID'd myself as "Dustin 'I own Mike Lowell in cribbage' Pedroia." Mike was *pissed*. He got a book from some cribbage expert and studied up on it. Then he beat me the next eight times we played.

I should also say that Mike Lowell is by far the best Ping-Pong player on our team, and possibly in the world. I'll give him that— but I'm a damn close second. He kicked my ass in Cleveland in 2007. He beat me twenty-nine straight times.

I'm not joking when I say that Mike Lowell doesn't need to be playing baseball. He could retire and play Ping-Pong profession-ally. He's a two-time World Series champion, a World Series MVP, a four-time All-Star, a Gold Glove and Silver Slugger winner, and has the best fielding percentage of all time for third basemen. But I'm telling you, he's playing the wrong sport.

In my routine, I played cribbage with Tito before every game. It wasn't a superstition, it was a ritual. It was one more part of the routine that got me ready to play.

Most days, after cribbage, I'd have an energy drink to get the blood flowing. I'd lift weights once a series. If it was my lifting day, I would go ahead and do that right away. If not, I would just hang out, reading the paper or watching TV.

At two o'clock, it was time to go upstairs and eat lunch.

At 2:30, I'd go do my flips and my tee work with Dave Magadan. For that, Dave will stand behind a pitching screen at short range in the cage and throw underhand flips to me; then I'll hit balls off the batting tee.

Now it was 3:30, less than three hours to game time. That's when I'd go out and do my ground balls. Last year, first-base coach Luis Alicea would hit balls to me. I had my specific routine there. I'd always try to take between thirty and forty ground balls every day. I liked to take my ground balls before batting practice; that way I wouldn't have to be dodging balls while people were hitting. That can turn into a circus, so I tried to avoid that.

I'd do ground balls for about half an hour, then when batting practice started at 4:25 I'd chill out in the dugout for half an hour, talking shit at the media people who were around, and just having fun.

Next I took my batting practice. It was now five o'clock, two hours before the game. Then down to the clubhouse. I'd take off my uniform and put on some shorts, go upstairs again, eat, and then go in the whirlpool for five minutes. Then I would take a shower, put on my uniform, and head down to the batting tunnel. Six o'clock now, just one hour and five minutes to game time.

I'd then listen to the pregame report on NESN, just to see what those guys were talking about, until Dave Magadan came back down to the tunnel at 6:15. Mags and I would do more flips. After I'd hit, I would go up to the dugout and sit for ten minutes. I'd stretch from 6:40 to 6:45, then play catch from 6:45 until 6:50.

Ten minutes more, and I would be taking the field for the national anthem.

I've gotten into habits that create a feeling of being comfortable. People have commented on how I tighten my batting gloves after every pitch. The fact is that I'm really not even aware of it. Because my hands are smaller, I have to cinch the gloves to get them the way I want, but I'm also thinking about the at-bat.

There was one weird thing a lot of people wanted to know about in the 2008 season. People kept asking me, and I wouldn't say, and that made people more curious: What did I put in my helmet after I got on base?

On May 23, we were playing in Oakland and I dove for a ball and sprained my thumb pretty badly.

When I swung the bat, it hurt a little bit, but I thought, Well, whatever. I was taking batting practice, but I wasn't swinging the bat really hard because I didn't want to test it and make it worse than it was. I wanted to make sure I could play through it.

But a few days later, we had a game in Baltimore, and we were facing Daniel Cabrera. In my first swing against him that game, I got jammed so bad that I bone-bruised the other hand.

The next three weeks, it was pure hell. Tito said, "Hey, you can rest." But I didn't want to.

I continued to play, but it was tough. I'd been hitting about .300 on May 23, and two weeks later, by June 6, I was down in the .260s. I went something like 5 for 70. My hands didn't just hurt, they wouldn't work.

Our trainer, Paul Lessard, was trying everything. I played for a while with a thumb guard on my glove hand, and I was taping my thumb, but it was still hurting.

Paul had me put this sticky shock-absorbing gel pad on my left thumb, and told me to deal as best I could with the pain in my right thumb, and I'd be able to swing fine. However, it was my left thumb that felt like it was about to fall off. Still, my right thumb was the one that was big and bruised, and the pad evened it out a bit so I could swing better.

Once I started using that gel pad, when I got jammed swinging on a pitch, I couldn't feel it very much. I felt it, but it wasn't doing any damage to my bone. It wouldn't bruise it to where I couldn't move.

I started using that, and when I'd get a hit, I'd take it off and put it in my helmet. I'd stick it on the inside so I wouldn't lose it before I got up to bat the next time. Once my thumb got healthy, which was a little less than a month later, I continued to use it, just in case it happened again. Strangely enough, my left thumb seemed to heal at the same time as the right one, over two to three weeks altogether.

People began asking me what it was I put in my helmet when I got on base. I told them, "None of your business." People were saying I was slumping again, and all this other shit, but it hurt! I didn't want anybody to know that. I didn't want to sit there like I was making excuses. After all, it's just a part of an everyday player's job. You're supposed to play hurt. If everybody felt great all year, everybody would rake. It's just a given that if I have to, I go out there and play hurt for my team. The reporters and the fans don't need to know every little injury a player has, because everybody who plays gets those kinds of injuries. I don't want anybody feeling sorry for me. I'm here to win baseball games. I'm not here just to play when everything feels 100 percent fine.

It was funny, all the interest in that. It became a mystery.

People thought it was a weird superstition of some kind, and the less I talked about it, the more people asked me. But it was really nothing.

MY ROUTINE WOULD always continue after the game, too. I'd come in and get out of my uniform and eat dinner. After dinner, I'd go downstairs and take my shower. If I needed to talk to the media that day, I'd do that while I put my clothes on, and then head home.

Once I got home, it would take me about two hours to wind down. Kelli and I usually just hang out and watch TV. We don't really talk much about the game. When I come through the door, she might say, "Great game!" and then that's pretty much it.

I love watching reality shows, so Kelli would have them recorded so we'd watch them together for a couple of hours. But the third hour, I'd be watching *Baseball Tonight*. I'd sit there in front of the TV talking shit at Orel Hershiser and Fernando Vina and Eduardo Perez. I'd sit there laughing at stuff and talking back at my TV screen.

Last year, as we got deeper in the season and we were in a race, it became tougher to wind down. If we lost a game 2-1 and I had two strikeouts and they scored the game winner on my error, I'd stay up all night thinking about it, about my at-bats, or those ground balls coming off a bat at me, or about how I was going to get on base the next game.

But it's also a job, and in any job anybody has, there are days that just aren't going to be great. Playing baseball, and taking all the ups and downs that go with it, that's my gig. Just like all the other parts of the routine of the day, failure is part of the day—baseball is a game built on failing more than you succeed.

And you have to be ready for the next day. It's late by the time I turn off the TV, and by the time I'm ready to go to bed, it's 1:30, maybe 2.

That's how it is. That's my day, every single day in the season.

I talk to my dad just about every day on the phone. At spring training I call him first thing in the morning, and in the season it's whenever I get up. He's a calming influence on me. We talk and it helps get my mind in the right place. Anybody who's ever met him knows what I'm talking about. He's been a great father to me, and he's worked his butt off for the family, and he's always taught me to respect people. Talking to him every day reminds me of how I should try to be as a person.

Adam Speakman

Red Sox Fan

I've always been short, and I've always been a second baseman. From the time I started playing baseball there always seemed to be an unspoken understanding that the only kids who ever really make it are the big kids. Because I was always smaller, I never had the strength or the natural athletic talent of most of my peers. To be successful to any degree, I had to hustle and play hard and play scrappy.

I grew up with the Red Sox in my blood. My grandparents worshiped Ted Williams as a god, and used to see Red Sox games when tickets cost fifty cents. When my mother was a young girl they would bring her to the Sox spring training in Florida. Baseball was the sport of choice in my family's house, and the Red Sox were the team. By the time I was born, my entire family already had a permanent relationship with the Boston Red Sox.

My grandmother was a devout and original member of the BoSox Club. She joined when it started in 1967. Through the club, she would get all of her grandchildren tickets every year. Summer to summer, the Red Sox were a constant among all the kids of my family.

My grandmother died recently. In her first seventy-three years of life she never saw the Red Sox win the World Series. In her last five years, she saw them win twice. Both times were among the happiest I've ever seen her. When we gathered for her funeral, there was a Red Sox balloon and a picture of Ted Williams near her ashes. My grandfather, her husband of fifty-five years, was dressed in his finest Sox shirt.

I first saw Dustin Pedroia in person on a muggy summer day in 2006 at Fenway. My brother, Jason, and I were going to go down to Pesky's Pole to try to catch batting practice home runs. But instead, because of the heat, we sat in the shaded box seats high up behind home plate where we had a good view of all the Red Sox hitters. We watched Lowell and Ortiz launch balls into the bullpen and up on the Monster. We saw Youk hit screaming line drives all over the field. And then Dustin Pedroia stepped into the box. I ran right down to the edge of the field, as close as I could get. I wanted to watch this small guy with this great big swing take his hacks at the ball. He pounded pitch after pitch after pitch. There was a moment for me of confirmation. Dustin was going to start that day for the Red Sox. Someone my height was about to play in a big-league game.

The most popular players in my childhood were the kings of the steroid era. The best players were all big, hulking hitters, guys who were massive and muscular and lived to hit bombs. It was difficult for a small kid who played defense and mostly picked up singles to idolize a masher.

Someone like Dustin, who lacks the physical build of his team-mates, has to play bigger than himself. You can see it when he runs out ground balls or ranges for a play in the gap. The extra effort, the last-second dive, the scrappiness. I still vividly remember watching the bounding ball that was going to take the no-hitter away from Clay Buchholz before Dustin, sprawling in the dirt, made a game-saving play.

I'm a freshman in college. I'm a second baseman for the team at Emerson College in Boston. I'm one of the smallest players on the team, but that's nothing new. I play the same position in the same city as Dustin—from my school, you can see the light of Fenway in the sky at night. And we happen to be the same size. When he won Rookie of the Year, it gave me more confidence, just to know that someone in the exact same position as myself made it at the highest level. Not just the mashers. Dustin Pedroia brought baseball back to a human scale for me.

16

What Sophomore Jinx?

By the 2008 season, I felt like I could really let my personality be what it was, and that included stuff I would say out on the field. Mostly it's to loosen things up and get people to relax.

You try to have fun. The game's so stressful. Baseball is built around failure: even if you're a great hitter, you fail seven times out of ten. I know that and understand that. During pitching changes, the infielders all talk, and you have to have some fun. Alex Cora says the funniest thing I ever said was that I'm good-looking.

I joke around with the fans, too. Kids are always screaming at me. Some ten-year-old with a camera is yelling, "Hey, Pedroia, turn around!" I'll yell, "Hey, kid, shut up . . . Where are your manners?" I'll give it back to them and they seem to think it's funny.

When I came to the Red Sox, I didn't know much about the history of the organization. Being from the West Coast, it was all about the Giants. One example was Bobby Doerr, who had played second base with the Red Sox from 1937 to 1951, and is in the Hall of Fame. Bobby wore the number 1, now retired by the Red Sox.

In August 2007, they had Bobby Doerr Day at Fenway, and I got to meet him. He was eighty-nine years old. That day, he pulled me aside and we had a great talk. He told me he still watched every game, and said, "Don't ever let anyone try to change the way you play the game of baseball. You keep doing what you're doing." That meant a lot.

I learned that in Boston, it's important to know and understand the tradition, and to be a part of it.

Another ritual for me is talking every day with Johnny Pesky, who played shortstop for the Red Sox in the 1940s and '50s and has become a fixture with the team. I think that ever since that day Johnny watched me take batting practice in 2004, he has seen a lot of himself in me. I get on him all the time. He keeps thinking I'm from Oregon, when it's Jacoby Ellsbury who is. Johnny is from Oregon, and I think he's just claimed me for his home state.

Johnny had come up to the Red Sox in 1942, and he'd batted .331 his rookie year. He would have been the Rookie of the Year if that award had existed back then, and he was third in MVP voting. But the war was on, so he served in the navy for the next three years before coming back in '46. He had a great career, and then he managed and coached. Johnny always has something good to say, and something useful.

He wasn't very big—just like me. You can see why he sees a little bit of himself in me. We're both about the same size. He tries to tell me how to hit, and things like that.

He goes, "Ted Williams was the greatest hitter of all time . . ."

He says that over, and over, and over.

Now it's to a point where I'll say, "Johnny, I have to ask you a question. Who the hell is Ted Williams?"

I just like messing with him.

He'll say, "You little shit!"

It's all in good fun.

Johnny loves the game. That's what he knows. He's a throw-back-style player. He obviously played as hard as he could every game. When he watches the game, he's looking for those players who do that. The players who run every ground ball out, who dive for every ball, just the little things like that to help their team win. Johnny did that every single day he played the game.

I hope I can play the game just as hard as he did.

EVEN WITH THE fatigue from the Tokyo trip, I got off to a better start than I had in 2007. A month into the season, on April 22, we beat the Angels at Fenway 7-6, and I went 4 for 5 to bring my average to .364.

The second month, though, I began getting beat up. I bruised my ribs, sprained my left thumb, and bruised my right thumb. Everybody hits those stretches where you're beat up, and you keep playing every day. You're not performing at your highest level of ability, but you just keep on going.

I struggled. By June 1, I'd dropped down to .279. We were still winning, but something unexpected was happening. The Tampa Bay Rays were emerging. That was strange. They'd been in first place from the beginning of the season, after ten years of losing. They'd finished fifth out of five teams in the division every year but one, when they finished fourth.

It was weird for me to be in the big leagues and chasing a team. I hadn't had that experience in 2007. We kept fighting along, and I kept playing, and a little bit at a time my ribs healed, and my thumbs. I was hitting the ball well again, and we were winning.

On July 13, we were in first place, a half game up on the Rays, and that would be the last time. We stayed in second place in the division right until the end of the year. We were in good position for the wild card, and we were playing well, but we were having injury problems. Josh Beckett went down for a while, and Mike Lowell did, and we missed David Ortiz for two months. That's a big bat to have out of the lineup.

STEROIDS. WHEN OFFICIALS come in to do random testing, I understand why it's done, but when they ask me to pee in the cup, I always stand there and say, "Me? Are you serious?" I work out a lot and really try to get jacked for the season, but still, sometimes I'm accused of looking like the "before" photo.

In the minor leagues you get tested all the time, but after you get called up you get the random test.

I like to have fun with it. I'll go in there and they'll say, "Dustin, you've been randomly selected to be tested."

I'll say, "Are you shitting me? Why? Because I hit a home run last night? What the hell is this?"

And the guys will start laughing. They'll say, "Oh, you know we have a job to do."

I usually take my shirt off and flex for them a little bit and ask them if they seriously want me to pee in the cup. But all kidding aside, since I signed in 2004, and even through college and high school, there hasn't been a single time when I was offered steroids, or encouraged to take steroids, or heard anything about them. I think my age group must have missed it. We just weren't part of that era, at least from what I can see.

It's been tough seeing how the steroid situation has affected the game, and it was tough for me to see the whole issue play out with Barry Bonds. Here's my take on that whole steroid-era situation:

I grew up watching those guys and I watched Barry Bonds when he played for the Pirates and his first few years with the Giants. He was the best player in the game, hands down, for seven or eight years before any of this. Honestly, I don't know if he took steroids or what. I only know what everybody else knows. But if he did, he was a great player even before that.

Back in the late 1990s, all these guys started hitting loads of home runs. Guys like Mark McGwire and Sammy Sosa were hitting sixty and seventy home runs. Then Barry Bonds hit 73. In my opinion, Barry was the best player before the steroid era, and he's been the best player after the steroid era. There is no doubt in my mind. He's been the best player for fifteen straight years. I'm sure you could have asked a pitcher, "Who do you hate facing?" They would almost certainly have said Barry Bonds.

He hit .330 with forty home runs and 120 or 130 RBI every single year before all this nonsense of guys hitting seventy home runs came out.

In my mind that's a player who is going to help his team win, not a guy who just hits home runs. It was hard to see a guy I admired caught up in all that. I'd thought he was Superman.

But I feel like the steroids era ended before I got to the major leagues. All those big numbers were something that seems to be in the past.

A DEFINITE HIGHLIGHT of the season was Jon Lester's no-hitter against the Royals at Fenway on May 19. Jon's is an incredible story, and because he was another homegrown guy I'd been teammates with at every level of the minor leagues, it was all the more special.

Jon's experience, like Kelli's, is something that reminds you of the important things. Playing in a professional sport, and being the age we are, it can be easy to feel that things like that won't affect us. I remember what a shock it was to hear that Jon was ill. It happened in August 2006. Jon had started the season with the PawSox, as I did, and in June he'd been called up. He'd started strong, getting six wins and only two losses before his back began to hurt. He'd been in a car accident, just a fender bender—someone had rear-ended him on Storrow Drive in Boston as he was driving to Fenway for a game against the Yankees on August 18. That night, he pitched and had a rough outing in a game the Red Sox lost 14-11.

Over the next few weeks, he was in a lot of pain. His first thought was that the back pain was an effect of that accident.

I had just been called up, having joined the team three days earlier in Anaheim, on August 22. The next night, August 23, Jon got his seventh win against the Angels, in my second game in the big leagues. He was the youngest Red Sox pitcher to get seven wins since 1970. It was all happening—the guys I'd known in Portland and Pawtucket, we were here. Youk played third that night and Pap closed out the game.

But Jon's back pain wasn't getting better. He wasn't the type of guy to give in to pain—he was a big, strong kid from Tacoma who liked to hunt and fish. But on August 28, Jon was scratched from his scheduled start in Oakland against the Athletics. They sent him back to Boston for tests. The team came back to Boston for a four-game series with Toronto, and it was before the first game that they told us that the cause of Jon's pain wasn't the car accident, it was cancer. He had lymphoma.

I have a special kind of relationship with Jon Lester. I played with him at every level, and he had actually committed to go to Arizona State, so I always gave him a hard time about that—"Hey, why didn't you go to Arizona State . . . You signed with the Red Sox when you should have taken the scholarship . . ."

As we kept playing together, I could see the talent this guy had. When we were playing in Double A, everyone knew: this guy was going to be a number-one pitcher in a major-league team's rotation for a long, long time. Anybody who watched him day in and day out could see what kind of work ethic he had.

I ended up seeing him next at Fenway Park, in the parking garage. I could tell what had happened from the look on his face. It said, *I don't know what to do.*

You never see weakness from Jon. I remember looking in his face and seeing him down, unsure and worried. To see Jon like that hurt me. Jon is an unbelievable person. He'll help you out in every way he can, in any way you need it. He was twenty-two years old and had everything coming down on him.

Jon went right into his treatments, and it would be another eleven months before he pitched for the Red Sox again. His first game back was in Cleveland, and he pitched six innings, only allowed two runs, and got the win. For a lot of people, it would have been enough. But in the 2007 World Series, Jon was on the mound for Game Four, pitching into the sixth inning, not allowing a run, and getting the win as we clinched the World Championship. That would have been enough, too.

Jon always has great stuff, but it seemed that he had a little more on the ball than normal. I remember sitting in the dugout in the first couple of innings. Normally, I would always make comments to him, just doing what I could to keep him going. But that night, I remember walking by him and deciding not to. I could see he was really focused and locked in. As the game went on, he just kept getting stronger and stronger. I was thinking, I can't believe what's going on right now. We had seen Clay Buchholz throw a no-hitter the previous year, but we understood this was going to be different because of what Jon had gone through in his life, and how he overcame everything.

When Jon walked out for the ninth, Fenway was as loud as I've heard it. When he finished the game by blowing a 94-mile-per-hour fastball past Alberto Callaspo, everybody went crazy. It was the eighteenth no-hitter thrown by a Red Sox pitcher. I feel like I was on the field for two of the most incredible of those—Clay Buchholz's, in the second big-league start of his career, and Jon Lester's, coming back from all that he had gone through. Jon will be a great pitcher with the Red Sox for a long time, and anybody who saw what he went through has to feel good about that.

It was just one of those games. Jon Lester was a cancer survivor before this, and he was getting back to being a major leaguer; and after this game he took himself from being a good major-league pitcher to being one of the best in the game. And I think everybody in the whole stadium knew that, and were watching it happen. He grew up right in front of us, and we knew he was going to be special for a long, long time. I'm proud to be his teammate.

I had experienced so much worry because of Kelli having melanoma at such a young age, but Kelli and Jon are both strong-minded people. They feel like they can beat anything. I think when you're going through something like that, you have to think that way. Jon never talks about it. He never wants anyone to feel sorry for him. He just wants to show everybody that if he can do it, anybody can do it.

WE HAD A ton of adversity, with one injury after another, and then there was the Manny situation.

I was a little upset with how things transpired. I also knew I was not the one to say, "Hey, Manny, pick it up." That was not my responsibility, yet. Three years before I'd been this kid walking up to him in the Best Buy in Fort Myers telling him what a big fan I was. So I knew my place.

Throughout the whole situation, I tried to stay exactly the same toward Manny as I always had been. I supported him, and I always support every one of my teammates. But I knew he wasn't happy. Anyone could tell that. It wasn't the Manny Ramirez we all had gotten to know and love, smiling and joking around. Everyone knew that he didn't want to be there. All you had to do was look at him. I think it was upsetting, and not just to me as a younger guy on the team, but to everybody on the team who valued Manny as a teammate and a friend.

We all loved Manny. Under those circumstances it's unfortunate he had a run-in with the front office over his contract. We did our best to just get out and do what we needed to do on the field without letting the situation have a negative effect. We had every intention of repeating as World Series champions, and that meant going out every day and doing our job to the best of our ability.

And in the same way, even though he was unhappy, none of us

took it as a personal thing toward us. Manny loved his teammates. It just became clear he needed to look for something else, and it wasn't about us during that time.

The incident in late June in Houston, where he shoved traveling secretary Jack McCormick, created a lot of attention. Manny had apparently gotten upset with Jack regarding a last-minute request for tickets, and pushed Jack, who is in his sixties, down to the floor.

I didn't see the incident. I was hitting at the time. But what I can say about Jack McCormick is that he's a first-class gentleman and has helped me and my family out more than anyone in the Red Sox organization. This guy makes sure I only have to worry about one thing, and that's playing baseball. He'll do anything for anybody. There couldn't be a better guy working in the job Jack does. I think it was an unfortunate incident and that in hindsight it would have been handled differently on both sides, because I'm sure Manny regrets what he did. I haven't ever really talked to Jack about it, but I'm sure Jack's sorry about it ever becoming an issue. But I don't think Jack has anything to be sorry about in the way he handled himself.

A little bit more than a month later, Manny was traded.

We also saw guys step up. Kevin Youkilis was playing better than ever, and Jon Lester was following that no-hitter by continuing to have a great year. I sensed that I had to do a little extra because of the guys who were out. Julio Lugo got hurt, so Jed Lowrie was called up from Pawtucket. He'd been up a bit in April, when Mike Lowell was out, and now he was back to play for Julio. Here was a new, young shortstop, who'd never played that position in the big leagues, getting put right into a pennant race.

There come those times in a long season when you feel broken down, and you have to fight through it. I feel like part of what has made me a good player is mental toughness, the determination to bounce back when things are difficult. There are times during the season when no matter how much you love the game, you're thinking, This sucks. I can't wait until the end. It's a long journey. It's 162 games. Anybody can feel good during the tenth game of the season, but what about game 100 or game 161? I believe that's when you show what kind of man and what kind of player you can be.

Every guy had to do his part. With Mike Lowell out, Youk moved over to third, and Sean Casey played first base, but then Sean hurt his neck in late August and Jeff Bailey came in to play first base. J. D. Drew, after catching fire and going nuts for a while, got hurt, and in came Mark Kotsay. There were things going on. Jacoby went to right field some games and Coco Crisp would be in center field. We would have different lineups on different days to try to deal with all the injuries. And we continued to find a way to win.

IN JULY, I got exciting news. I had been voted the starting second baseman for the American League All-Star Team. Our team also put Manny in left field, and Youk was voted in at first base. The All-Star Game was at Yankee Stadium that year, and the left side of the infield would be A-Rod at third base and Derek Jeter at shortstop.

I was glad I would be there for the last All-Star Game in a place with the kind of history that Yankee Stadium has. To have the infield made up of two Yankees and two Red Sox added to the sense of fun. Two guys on one side of the infield who had been can't-miss players since birth, and a couple of dirt dogs like Youkilis and me on the other.

Youk deserves all the credit for not only being such a great player, but for being the guy who set the tone for all the homegrown guys with the Red Sox. He was up there before me, Pap, Lester, Manny Delcarmen, Brandon Moss, all the guys who came up and played together. I remember reading all these articles that said he was the "Greek God of Walks," all that kind of stuff. He's definitely an on-base guy. But I remember getting a chance to play with him at Triple A and watching him, thinking, This guy is definitely not looking to walk. He can flat-out hit. His intensity toward the game was something to see. It didn't matter if he was playing first or third base; he was always diving around and always cared about one thing: winning. As a player and especially as a teammate, you respect the fact that he leads by example, and so everybody wants to play that way.

Youk is a huge reason why the Red Sox give all these young guys a chance. He came up through the Red Sox minor-league system and was able to perform well in Fenway, and he's going to do it for a lot longer than the four years he's had so far.

As far as the rivalry with the New York Yankees goes, it's a lot of fun playing against those guys. You look out there, and heck, eight of their nine starters are borderline Hall of Famers. I think going into the Stadium always elevates your game. They've won the most championships of all time. If you can't get up for playing a game against the Yankees, there's no chance you're getting up for much of anything. And being in the division, we get a chance to do it eighteen times a year. That's pretty special. The fans love it and each city loves it. For the players there's nothing like going out there and competing against the best, and both of our teams have great track records. The rivalry is special and hopefully it will continue to get better and better. At the All-Star Game, I was a teammate of Derek Jeter. I always had a lot of respect for him. We got a chance to talk and get to know each other.

Jeter has won four championships and is the poster boy for being a Yankee. That's something people look up to. He's the man. I have never heard anyone say anything bad about Derek Jeter, that's for sure. He's a proven winner. Why wouldn't I try to get a tip or two from a guy who is known for being a winner? That's exactly what I'm trying to be, someone like him. I was like a sponge around him during the All-Star Game, listening to what he had to say and trying to pick his brain about everything. I took a few things from him that have already helped me become a better player.

Playing in my first All-Star Game was pretty special. When I came out on the field, there were All-Stars out there from past years, as well as National League starting second baseman Chase Utley. For my grand entrance, all the fans at Yankee Stadium booed me as loud and as long as they could. That was cool. I guess you have to figure that if Yankees fans boo you that loudly, it's a measure of the amount of respect they have for you.

I had never been to an All-Star Game before and didn't know what to expect. The Yankees did a great job the whole weekend. Tito was there, along with all of our coaching staff. I got to share the experience with a lot of teammates. The Red Sox also had Jason Varitek, Jonathan Papelbon, and J. D. Drew on the All-Star roster.

We dressed in the Yankees' clubhouse, which some Yankees fans made a big deal about. Personally, I didn't care. I just wanted to play the game. I would have been just as excited to get dressed in Seattle's locker room. As long as I'm in a locker room, putting on my uniform and getting a chance to play baseball, I don't give a shit where it is. Still, it was cool to see the inside of the Yankees club-house. They had those "NY" logos all over the place and the tops of the lockers looked like the façade at the top of the stadium.

As for the game, the American League won in fifteen innings, 4-3. It was nearly two in the morning when the game ended. J. D. was named the game's Most Valuable Player after he hit a two-run homer in the seventh inning to tie the game. Then it was back to join the team at Anaheim.

JULY TURNED TO August, then September. The season was going by fast, but slow. We were in second place, slowly grinding it out, and we thought we could catch Tampa Bay. We were just hoping we wouldn't run out of games too quickly before we could do that.

As we got toward the end of the season, Joe Mauer of the Twins and I were right at the top of the stats for batting, separated by a point or two. But rather than thinking much about a batting title, I didn't really care. By the end of the season I'd only missed three games, even playing with some injuries through the year that are part of an everyday player's job. We had clinched for the playoffs, so Tito came to me and he said, "Listen, I know what's going on, and I'd like to give you a day or two off, to get healthy for the playoffs. How do you feel about that?"

I could have said, "Hell no, I want to play those games and try to win the batting title," but our first priority as a team from day one was to accomplish the goal of repeating as World Champions.

If I'm beat-up and hurt, and I can't play 100 percent because I'm after some individual success, then I'm not helping the team, I'm hurting it.

So I sat two of the last three games. I ended up hitting .326 and Joe got on a hot streak and ended up at .328. But I was happy that I'd hit well to help the team. I wanted to come home and tell my friends we were World Series champions, not that I won a batting title.

There was also talk of both Youk and me being potential Most Valuable Player candidates. Given the way we play together, and the relationship we have, and the fact that the main goal for both of us was to win another World Series, there was no competition between us on that. It was obviously a great honor, but we weren't losing sleep over it. Youk was having a great season, and there were many things he did to help the team win. When Mike Lowell was hurt, Youk went over to third base and played great at that position, because he always puts the team first. In the end, Youk was just as deserving as I was to win the award. If you win awards you win them, and if you don't, you don't. I don't set out to play for a batting title or the MVP. I set out, as everybody on the team does, to win it all, as a team.

WE KEPT PLAYING, but in the end there weren't enough games. Tampa Bay finished two games up on us. But we got the wild card, and again in 2008, we were facing the Angels in the American League Division Series. And given what we'd been through with injuries, getting into the playoffs was what mattered.

I had hit well in 2008. But all that was done, and now it was the postseason, where everything starts fresh. And we figured if we could have everyone reasonably healthy, we'd have a chance. We definitely felt like we could still win it all.

But we had to get by the Angels first, and they'd been the best team in baseball the whole year. They'd won their division by twenty-one games. Their pitching staff was dominant, and as the wild-card team, we were going on the road.

The first two games of the series were out in Anaheim, and there were a lot of people wondering if we were going to come back to Fenway two down. But in Game One, Jon Lester pitched a great game and we won 4-1. Then people were saying they'd be happy if we came back home with the series tied. But Dice-K pitched really well in Game Two, and we won 7-5.

Game Three was back at Fenway, and everybody knew the Angels were too good not to fight back hard. Josh Beckett was pitching, and it was a tight game. The lead went back and forth, and we went into extra innings tied at 4-4. I was struggling. In the bottom of the tenth I struck out, and in the bottom of the eleventh I came up with Coco on second base and a chance to win the game, but grounded out to third.

In the top of the twelfth, with Mike Napoli having singled and then moved to second on a bunt by Howie Kendrick, Erick Aybar singled to bring him in. In the bottom of the twelfth, after Jeff Weaver walked David Ortiz to start things off, we went down 1-2-3.

I'd gone 0 for 13 to start off the playoffs. We'd had a couple of days off before the series, and that's always tough for me. I was out of my rhythm. My timing was off just a little bit, but that was enough. If your timing is just a little bit off, you're going to get overmatched by the kind of pitching you're facing when you're in the playoffs. I sat in our apartment after we lost Game Three, and told Kelli I needed to do something.

"I've helped our team win the whole season," I said, "and this isn't the time for me to be going into a funk."

The next night, we beat the Angels with Jon Lester back on the mound. He was pitching really well.

In the bottom of the fifth, I did something to help. I doubled to left off John Lackey to bring in Jason Varitek from second and put us up 2-0.

Lester pitched seven innings of shutout ball, and when he left the game, we still had that 2-0 lead. But we gave up two in the eighth, and it was still tied up 2-2 as we went into the bottom of the ninth. Jason Bay doubled, and with two outs, Jed Lowrie put a ground ball into right field to bring in Bay for the win. Again, it was a situation where everyone on the team was contributing. We'd beaten a very tough Angels team.

NOW WE WERE in the ALCS with the Rays. It was a mentally draining series. We'd fought the whole year to try to get to this point, through all kinds of injuries, and you could see that everybody was beat up and worn out. I felt like that extra month, beginning the season in Tokyo, had killed us.

We were running on empty. We were playing all on heart. You could see guys like Beckett out there fighting through an oblique injury, and Lester was beat up after pitching two games of the four against the Angels. Mike Lowell tried to play through his hip injury, and he just couldn't.

But we made it a series. In Game One at Tropicana Field, Dice-

K pitched a great game, giving up four hits in seven innings, and we won 2-0. I got a single, then scored the second run when Youk doubled.

Game Two was crazy. I'd finally gotten my timing back. I hit a home run to left to lead off the third and tie the game 2-2, and then I hit another home run to lead off the fifth and put us one run behind in an inning that ended up with us ahead 6-5. Both home runs were off Scott Kazmir. But with the score 8-8 in the bottom of the eleventh, B. J. Upton hit a sacrifice fly to bring in Fernando Perez to win.

The game had gone on for five and a half hours.

BACK AT FENWAY two nights later, everything felt strange. Jon Lester, who'd been asked to do so much, struggled that night. We got behind 5-0 in the first few innings, and Tampa added three more in the eighth, and in the end we lost 9-1. We were down in the series 2-1.

The next night, Game Four, it was the same thing. This time Wake was pitching, and we were down 11-1 by the end of the sixth.

We lost the game 13-4. Everything felt tired, the effects of a long season. I was getting my hits—after Game Four I was hitting nearly .500—but it wasn't making a lot of difference.

Game Five at Fenway, with us down in the series 3-1, started out just as badly. We were down 5-0 after three, and by the bottom of the seventh inning, it was 7-0. I saw something then that I'd never seen before: people got up and started leaving Fenway Park.

Some of the fans thought it was over, but we didn't. In the bottom of the seventh, Jed doubled to lead off, then Coco singled. I got up and sent a line drive into right center to score Jed and put

Coco on third: 7-1. Then David Ortiz, who'd had such a tough year with injuries, hit a bomb out to right and it was 7-4.

With Tampa's bullpen having been lights out all year, it still wasn't looking too good. But you could see some people coming back down to their seats.

We came up in the eighth inning and Jason Bay walked to start things off. Then J. D. Drew hit a home run to make it 7-6. Kotsay doubled, and then Coco got a humongous single to bring him in. Going into the ninth, it was tied up. It was just good at-bat after good at-bat. We were beginning to think, Could all this be meant to happen again?

We ended up winning the game in the bottom of the ninth when J. D. singled to score Youk.

After the game, I was all fired up. I had packed my bags for Tampa and brought them to the field. I mean, when I packed that day, I had decided I was going to Tampa, regardless. Win or lose, I'd already decided I was headed to Tampa for *something,* even if I didn't know exactly what. There was no way I was going back to the apartment that night, because I wouldn't let myself even consider the possibility.

I went into the wives' lounge after the game, and I was so excited, and everyone was *quiet.* I was joking around and trying to talk, and this place was like a church.

I was thinking, What's going on? We'd just won. What the hell was going on?

Ashley Papelbon, who's not afraid to talk, said, "Hey Pedey, when we were down 7-0, Kelli went ahead and booked your flight back to Arizona."

Kelli had started making the arrangements. She said that the second she pushed "Purchase," the comeback began.

I looked at her, shaking my head, and I said, "Wow, you weren't believing . . ."

I don't want to throw my wife under the bus for doing that, but I'll kind of gently roll her under the bus. That night, what I was thinking was, It seems like I always have to be trying to motivate somebody to *believe*. But that was how it was all feeling. Usually it's not my wife, because she's awesome. But what can I say? That time it was.

WE WENT BACK down to Tampa with the series 3-2, Tampa Bay. On the overnight flight to Tampa, we were asking ourselves, "How the hell did we just win that game?" No one was sleeping on that flight. Everyone was all fired up.

Beckett was pitching Game Six at Tropicana. And everybody knew from his past what he was capable of doing. But he was also hurt. Everyone knew it.

He went out there and he just *pitched*. Even in pain, at the end of a tough, long season, he hung in there for five innings and got the win, 4-2. We were going to a Game Seven.

GAME SEVEN. WE'D fought the entire season to get back to that point, to have a chance to get back to the World Series. Jon Lester threw a great game that night, but we just got shut down. I hit a home run in the first inning to put us up 1-0, but it became clear it just wasn't our time. Matt Garza had it that night, pitching seven solid innings.

That was the end. We watched the Rays celebrating, and I had that feeling of putting so much effort into something but in the end being unsatisfied.

If you're going to win a championship, you need to have some breaks. We hadn't. The season had started so early, and there had been freak injuries to people, and it seemed like everybody was hurting. But I'd always believed that in some ways you make your own breaks, and I was proud of how we'd fought back.

Mike Lowell

Third Baseman

Boston Red Sox

My first impression of Dustin Pedroia was not a good one.

I came over from the Florida Marlins in 2006, and when I arrived at spring training I was meeting people, asking, "Who's this guy?" and "Who's that guy?" just to get to know my new teammates. Someone pointed and said, "Oh, and this is our second-rounder."

Pedey was standing there, and he looked overweight. I thought, I didn't know they gave short fat people such big ceilings to get drafted so high.

After I got to know him, I got to know that his personality is very dry humor. And he has a chip on his shoulder. After I saw the way he approached the game, I really liked it.

One thing that sticks out in my head is when he would get hits, he would come into the dugout and say, "Yeah, yeah, you guys saw that rocket."

I said, "Who is this guy?" I remember that I didn't say a word when I was a rookie in the big leagues or in a big-league camp. But I think he feels like he basically had to be that guy, because that's the way he is, even when he's in a different environment.

I think his story is outstanding.

He's the type of guy who, I can guarantee, no one gave any credit to, just by looking at him. No one would give him credit to be a big-leaguer, let alone Rookie of the Year, let alone the MVP of the American League. It's pretty remarkable what he's been able to accomplish in that short time.

You can see he wants to work hard and stay at that level. He's not saying "Hey, I've made it now, and I've got a nice contract" and shutting it down. He's looking to improve upon those numbers and really be a good player for a lot of years.

And he's got a million stories.

My favorite was when they didn't let him in at Coors Field in Colorado for the World Series, and he told them to ask Jeff Francis to identify him.

That epitomizes his personality.

I tried to give him encouragement when I could, just drawing on my own experiences.

For example, he got hot and was getting two or three hits a game for about five or six games. He had been struggling and hitting under .200 but all of a sudden he's up to .240 or .250, which is respectable. I just wanted to tell him, "Don't be complacent with .240 or .250 just because you've proved you can get as hot as anyone for five days."

So you just keep pushing.

Once the playoffs are over and the season ends, you can totally shut her down. But I think a lot of guys, when they go through a stretch when they're really hot for two weeks, begin to think, Well, even if I go 1 for my next 10 I'm still hitting X . . . So why are you going to sell yourself short by going 1 for 10? Why not go 4 for 5, or 5 for 10? There's a reason why you got so hot: you're doing good things and you're seeing the ball well.

I've also told Pedey to try to prolong the good stretches as long as he can. And when there are bad stretches, to get out of them as soon as he can. That sounds easy, but it's hard to do. You have to learn to think a certain way.

By with the style he plays and the way he plays, I think people now realize he never lets down—ever.

Teammates appreciate that. Fans appreciate that. Everyone around the game does, too.

I don't know if he's going to be an MVP every year, but he's going to be an elite player every year because pitchers will always make the mistake of trying to throw fastballs by him. Physically guys still don't believe it. He has that ability to square the ball up as well as anyone. His consistency in putting the good part of the barrel on the ball is as good as anyone's in the league.

It's a shame in a way, because you want him to be six foot four and 220 pounds, just to see what he could really do by having so much more *umph* behind him. But I think his size adds to his mystique: How can a little guy swing so hard but still barrel up the ball so often?

That's what guys love about him.

17

MVP

And now it was another off-season.

My contract negotiations were happening, too. My agent and the Red Sox had started talking in August, but no offer was made at that time. The Red Sox waited until the off-season.

It was something I wanted to just get done. It's easier to go out there and play when you're just playing to win, when you're not playing for a contract. Obviously, I first and foremost have to think about taking care of my family. I love my teammates, but I want to be able to look after my wife and my mom and dad and my wife's family.

I also want to be here a long time. The Red Sox first offered me a five-year deal, and we sat on it for about a month, but in the meantime some things began to happen.

Those things were the Gold Glove, the Silver Slugger Award, and the Most Valuable Player Award.

At the end of the season, Kelli and I had planned to go on a vacation to Mexico, but we got a call from the Red Sox front office saying we should wait a few days until the MVP announcement came out. So we did. I had no idea how it would come out, but during that wait I thought about what had contributed to a good year.

I don't know if it had anything to do with the MVP, but I take a lot of pride in playing defense. I thought back on how in 2006 and 2007, it was the biggest part of my game when I first got called up. I wasn't hitting very well so I had to make sure to play great defense to stay in Boston. I work hard at it every day and try to find ways to get more range or get my arm stronger. I work just as hard on defense as I do on offense.

I also thought about how I'd committed over the last number of years to working on getting stronger and faster. I ate a lot less than I used to. I'd started to figure that out. I wasn't blessed with the best body in the world but I had committed to working on it, the hard way, which is to make small sacrifices. I cut out all the garbage. I like ice cream, and I never eat ice cream anymore and it sucks. But it's small things like that that you do just to get a little bit more improvement.

I thought about how the season ended, one game away from getting to the World Series. You put that in the front of your mind at the start of the off-season, that you have to work harder. The Rays were the best American League team of 2008, and who knows? Maybe the Rays just outworked us last off-season. But if I can have anything to do with it, no one is going to outwork our team. In the end you're supposed to be the strongest. Hopefully we did that in the off-season, and will do it every off-season.

When I got the call, I was home and Kelli was in the gym, working out. I called her, and when she answered, I said, "Do you remember how you said we'd be back at the Baseball Writers' dinner in New York again this winter?" She didn't remember. But I remembered how sure she had been when she said it.

WHEN THE ANNOUNCEMENT came that I'd won the Most Valuable Player Award for the American League, I felt unbelievably honored. I'd like to think it was a sign of the respect I had earned along the way. I'd gotten sixteen of the twenty-eight first-place votes, with Justin Morneau of the Twins second, and Youk third. In fourth place was the guy who had been the top draft pick in 2001, the year no one had even taken a chance on me—Joe Mauer.

The MVP award changed a lot of things. Going into my first full season in the big leagues, it was all about just proving I belonged on a major-league level. Then for my second year it was proving that the first year hadn't just been a fluke. Now it was about maintaining a level of play that could help get the Red Sox another World Series. That's the only goal. People ask me about personal goals and I say, "I haven't set any. I'm just here to do the same thing I've always done: play hard, get on base, score runs, and play great defense." I need to do everything I can to help us win. Those are my goals.

ALSO DURING THE 2008 season, talks for a contract extension began between the Red Sox and my agents, Sam and Seth Levinson.

I hadn't had that much leverage in negotiating when we began. I'm a guy with two years in the league, and guys with two years usually don't have any leverage when it comes to contract negotiations. My only leverage was, I'm the MVP of the American League.

My attitude to the Red Sox was, I'll give you a discount if you give me security. If you give me security, I'll never have to worry about money for the rest of my life. And the Red Sox did. They gave me a six-year deal for $40.5 million and a club option for another $11 million. Basically seven years and about $53 million, plus incentives: MVP voting results and that kind of stuff. What I gave up was the chance to have arbitration and then go into free agency.

I want to continue to get better as a player, but with the purpose being to help the team. Sometimes it's the intangibles that make a difference, and I felt that if the money was in place, that would be great, because I could focus more completely on the important goal: more championships for the Red Sox.

The off-season is always a chance to take some time to think about what it is you do, and why you do it. The biggest thing for me playing baseball, the biggest joy and the reason why I play, is to play for my team and my teammates.

These guys are your family. You are with them eight months out of the year. During the season you see your teammates more than you see your actual family. I play every day and I want to win for those guys. I've never played a meaningless season at ASU or with the Red Sox. Every game has counted from start to finish. I've never played a game where we were out of the pennant race and just finishing out the season. Every game is intense. That's what I live for.

I was fortunate enough to get drafted by the Red Sox, and to be able to play on a team where just about every player in that clubhouse thinks the same way. We put the team in front of ourselves. We've been successful doing that and we're going to continue to do that.

I couldn't have better teammates than I've had in Boston. Mike Lowell and Alex Cora are probably my two favorite teammates so far in my career. I've learned so much from both of them, including during my rookie season, when I'd watch the way they carry themselves. I don't think Mike gets enough credit for what he does, for being a great teammate and a great player and a winner. He didn't just help me play better when I was struggling, he helped me play better after I'd started playing better.

That rookie year, I had gotten out of my funk and was batting something like .310. Mike was sitting on the bench next to me and said, "Hey, listen . . ."

I said, "What?"

"Don't stop. Don't ever stop."

His way of playing tells you what he meant: don't ever let up. I was feeling good that I'd worked to a point where I was doing okay, and Mike knew it but also knew I needed that extra push, to say to myself that I wasn't going to let up, and that I was going to try to be even better.

He does stuff like that all the time, and sometimes I'm not even sure he knows he's doing it—it's just his natural way of being.

Mike Lowell is the kind of guy who makes you fifty times better as a person, just by being around him and his wife, Bertha, and their family. I don't think he gets enough credit for what he means to the success of the Red Sox.

At the beginning of the 2007 season, people were saying Alex Cora should be playing over me, and every single day I came in, Alex would say to me, "Work hard and you'll be fine. I've been where you are—I went through this when I came up in Los Angeles with the Dodgers. It's not easy."

Last year he said, "Man, when you came up I was trying to be really supportive, but I was beginning to think you couldn't play." But not once did I ever sense he felt that way. Every single day I came in and tried to work my butt off and he would teach me something new to help me get through the tough times. Now we're best friends. I'm texting or calling him every day, seeing how he's doing and how his family is doing. He was my locker mate for two years, and like an older brother to me. Without a doubt, when his playing career is over, he's going to be a manager or a coach, like his brother Joey, who's the bench coach for the White Sox under manager Ozzie Guillen. And I already told him that when I'm old and retired, I'll be his bench coach. He says when he manages, we'll be the opposite of Joey and Ozzie. Joey is calm and steady, and Ozzie is the emotional one. When we do it, Alex will be the calm, steady manager and I'll be the crazy bench coach.

MY RELATIONSHIP WITH my teammates is going to stay the same in a lot of ways. Everybody knows each other around here well enough; they know how I am. I don't need any special treatment. I'm just a normal guy. I'm not any different.

But I also remember the guys who treated me great when I walked into this clubhouse, so I definitely want to be one of those guys who treat newer players just as well.

I remember my first spring training game, playing against the Dodgers in Vero Beach. Everybody was fantastic to me right from the start. That's the way I'm going to treat all the younger players. That's part of being a veteran, and it's an attitude that can extend past my retirement as a player—hopefully a long time from now.

Epilogue

Today's Red Sox are different than most Boston teams of the past, and over the last few years, the fans have started to see that: it shows in the way we play the game. We show up, we play to win: that's all we care about. That's why a lot of other teams have complimented us. It's all rooted in the group of guys we have. We care about each other and we want everybody on the team to do well. We are here to win together.

These guys have my back and I love them. When I think of my teammates, it's more clear to me than ever that I was born to play this game.

I LOVE IT in Boston and my wife loves it, too. The team treats players' families unbelievably well. They make everything as easy as they can because the only thing they want you to worry about is baseball. You won't find that philosophy in many other places, from what I hear in talking to guys on other teams.

Playing in a huge media market like Boston has its negatives and its positives. On the negative side, you're under a microscope; everything you do is being watched. Everything your family does, or doesn't do, can be brought up. That part is difficult. I'm a really private person, as is Kelli, and we've become more private because of so much attention. A lot of people want to know what you do in your spare time, where you go, etc. The truth is, we don't do that much. Kelli and I try to keep our lives as quiet and low-key as possible.

The positive aspect of the huge media coverage is the way it draws attention to every player and every game. One of the perks of playing for the Red Sox is that we're on a national stage. It feels like we're on ESPN or Fox every other night. We're on Wednesdays and Saturdays and Sundays some weeks because we have a huge fan base. They're all over the world, what with the Japanese players who have come to the team. The exposure we get nationally is a lot more than other teams', and I'm thankful for that.

If you play well in this market, and the country likes the way you play the game, then you get rewarded for it. I think that's really helped me in my career. If it weren't for playing in Boston and having the fans we have, I don't think I would have been the MVP.

I'M IN A place where they've watched me grow up. They watched me through the minor leagues, and they saw me develop my skills at the major-league level. And they've come to learn that I'm a winner. In the clubhouse, I think they see me starting to become a leader.

The city of Boston embraces its team. There's nothing like seeing the fans happy when we do well.

Some people will say I signed for a discount, and I say, "No shit." I'm a realist. I look at the big picture and see it like it is. The money thing is an example. What can't I do with $40 million that I could do with $100 million? At some point you have to stop and say, "Listen, I'm a regular human being." Do I need a Bentley? Absolutely not. I don't care about those kinds of things.

But does this set my family and my kids up forever? Absolutely. There's no way in hell I could ever spend that kind of money. We already have a house, and it's all set up, and I wouldn't have any idea what to spend money on after that. The value to me is in being with this team. I love my teammates. Tito has been unbelievable to me, and so have Theo Epstein and the owners. The fans are awesome. Even when they were in my face, it was because they are passionate about this team like fans nowhere else.

There are some particular things that have meant a lot. For example, during that first month of my rookie year, when I was struggling, I was doing an autograph signing at a card show. This guy came up to me and said, "Hey, me and my kid are your biggest fans. I want you to write 'ROY 2007' on the ball."

ROY meant "Rookie of the Year."

I said, "Dude, I'm hitting like .150 right now. I'm probably the worst rookie that's ever been created."

He shook his head and said, "No, you just watch." He had played baseball in high school but had to work hard for any success. He seemed to identify with what I was going through.

So I wrote it on the ball. *ROY 2007.*

I told him, "Hey, if I win Rookie of the Year, I want that ball and then I'll sign another one for you."

Sure enough, I won the Rookie of the Year.

I saw him again at another card show. He had the ball with

him. He gave me the ball and I gave him another one, signed. He was happier than I was. He'd called it! That's the stuff that makes me happy. Even when there are ten people who hate you at the time, there's always one or two who believe in you and love you just for your effort. That was a turning point for me, that one fan, believing.

The fans become part of your life, like an extended family. You celebrate with them when things are going great, and sometimes you suffer their pain.

One thing that affected Kelli and me very deeply was when we were contacted by a doctor at Children's Hospital in Boston who told us about a couple who were devoted Red Sox fans. In the fall of 2007, they were expecting their second child. They decided, when the Red Sox got to the World Series, the way they would pick the boy's name: whoever the first Red Sox player was to hit a home run in the Series, that would be the baby's name if it was a boy. And then I led the Series off with a bomb.

The child that Kelli and I called "Baby Dustin" was born on January 21, 2008. But he was very ill, and for months none of the doctors could really come up with an answer.

Through the spring, Baby Dustin hung on. On May 19, Kelli and I went to Children's Hospital to see him and give whatever support and comfort we could to his parents.

Baby Dustin passed away two days later. The team was leaving on a road trip to the West Coast, so Kelli attended the services for both of us. We were so sad for that family, and what they had gone through.

I get a lot of letters from fans, and a lot of them seem to identify with me, or are encouraged by the way I've made it.

I hope that people can look at me and say, "This guy is a normal guy." When Kelli and I go to the mall, not a lot of people recognize me, which is just fine. I'm not going to big-league anybody. If you come up and talk to me, I'll sit down and talk with you for a minute, if I can.

I remember that flight from Ottawa to Anaheim, when I was traveling alone to become a major leaguer, and thinking that I wouldn't let them get me out of the uniform once I was in it. Now I see kids wearing their Pedroia jerseys. It's cool seeing people with my jersey on. The little kids wearing them, the jerseys hanging below their knees, that's good stuff. That makes me happy. If I see a little kid walking around with my jersey on, I know that means he relates to me and wants to be like me. Hopefully, he can grow up, work hard, and enjoy his goals in life, whatever they may be.

Boston has embraced me. I love playing here and that's why I'm going to be here for a long time.

No, I don't know what I'd spend money on. I could go out and buy expensive clothes, but the only clothes that ever feel completely right are the ones I wear playing baseball. The clothes I want to wear every day say "Red Sox," and those words go right over the heart.